Geographies of Media

Series Editors
Torsten Wissmann, Faculty of Architecture and Urban Planning,
University of Applied Sciences, Erfurt, Germany
Joseph Palis, Department of Geography, University of the Philippines
Diliman, Quezon, Philippines

Media is always spatial: spaces extend from all kinds of media, from newspaper columns to Facebook profiles, from global destination branding to individually experienced environments, and from classroom methods to GIS measurement techniques. Crucially, the way information is produced in an increasingly globalised world has resulted in the bridging of space between various scalar terrains. Being and engaging with media means being linked to people and places both within and beyond traditional political borders. As a result, media shapes and facilitates the formation of new geographies and other space-constituting and place-based configurations. The *Geographies of Media* series serves as a forum to engage with the shape-shifting dimensions of mediascapes from an array of methodological, critical and analytical perspectives. The series welcomes proposals for monographs and edited volumes exploring the cultural and social impact of multi-modal media on the creation of space, place, and everyday life.

Jörg Scheffer

Mirrored Spaces

Social Inequality in the Digital Age

Jörg Scheffer
Department of Geography
University of Passau
Passau, Germany

Geographies of Media
ISBN 978-3-658-42792-4   ISBN 978-3-658-42793-1   (eBook)
https://doi.org/10.1007/978-3-658-42793-1

Published with financial support from the University of Passau and the Open Access Publication Fund of University Library Passau

© The Editor(s) (if applicable) and The Author(s) 2020, 2024. This book is an open access publication.
This is the abridged and revised version of the book Digital verbunden—sozial getrennt. Social Inequality in Spatial Perspective (https://link.springer.com/book/10.1007/978-3-658-31110-0).

Open Access This book is licensed under the terms of the Creative Commons Attribution 4.0 International License (http://creativecommons.org/licenses/by/4.0/), which permits use, sharing, adaptation, distribution and reproduction in any medium or format, as long as you give appropriate credit to the original author(s) and the source, provide a link to the Creative Commons license and indicate if changes were made.
The images or other third party material in this book are included in the book's Creative Commons license, unless indicated otherwise in a credit line to the material. If material is not included in the book's Creative Commons license and your intended use is not permitted by statutory regulation or exceeds the permitted use, you will need to obtain permission directly from the copyright holder.
The use of general descriptive names, registered names, trademarks, service marks, etc. in this publication does not imply, even in the absence of a specific statement, that such names are exempt from the relevant protective laws and regulations and therefore free for general use.
The publisher, the authors, and the editors are safe to assume that the advice and information in this book are believed to be true and accurate at the date of publication. Neither the publisher nor the authors or the editors give a warranty, expressed or implied, with respect to the material contained herein or for any errors or omissions that may have been made. The publisher remains neutral with regard to jurisdictional claims in published maps and institutional affiliations.

Cover illustration: © Melisa Hasan

This Palgrave Macmillan imprint is published by the registered company Springer Fachmedien Wiesbaden GmbH, part of Springer Nature.
The registered company address is: Abraham-Lincoln-Str. 46, 65189 Wiesbaden, Germany

Paper in this product is recyclable.

Series Editors' Preface: Mirror, Mirror on the Wall...

Navigating social boundaries and ascending the socio-economic hierarchy has perennially posed a formidable challenge. Until the advent of industrialisation and changing societal structures, the tradition of a child's occupational succession, involving children inheriting and continuing their parents' professions or trades, was prevalent. However, this tradition gradually waned, giving way to more diverse and individualised career paths.

Contemporary youth have the freedom and liberty to select vocations aligned with their aptitudes and predilections, yet this premise is constrained by financial parameters and the intricate web of social and familial circumstances. Illustrative narratives (from J.D. Vance's political ascent in *Hillbilly Elegy* to Tom Ripley's aspirations for upward mobility in *The Talented Mr. Ripley*) delineate the influence of sociocultural demarcations on life trajectories. Long-standing thematisation within popular culture, exemplified by the 1987 film *Dirty Dancing* ("Nobody puts Baby in a corner"), has incessantly pointed out multiple entanglements impeding vertical mobility.

Mirrored Spaces delves into the convergence of financial and social disparities, expounding upon novel avenues of digital intervention that stand as prospective pathways to surmount societal constraints. The present book underscores the potential for an expanded array of options and opportunities within a digital society, while also casting scepticism whether digitalisation possesses the capacity to shatter the confines of social stratification. Studies reveal that the less privileged groups among young people use the internet and digital media in a consumerist and uncritical way, while those in the educated milieu perceive those resources as an expansion of their space in their search for further knowledge. As elucidated by Jörg Scheffer, social space and physical space retain significant meaning in virtual realms: "What a spatial perspective actually reveals is that the socially disadvantaged segments of the population are confronted with new reproductive mechanisms that solidify the status quo and cement social differences".

This perspective diverges from the outlook posited by Tobias Boos in the inaugural instalment of our Geographies of Media series. *Inhabiting Cyberspace and Emerging Cyberplaces* delineates the expansion of a sociocultural cluster's sphere of influence into the virtual expanse, transcending the confines imposed by geographical boundaries. This transposition willingly embraces sociocultural insulation to safeguard distinct cultural identities. However, as expounded by "Mirrored Spaces", the concomitant limitation of personalised digital space poses a deterrent to social progress, engendering an entrenched reinforcement of an individual's pre-existing habitus. What emerges as a boon for marginalised sociocultural groups, paradoxically undermines the holistic development of the individual.

The phenomena of stratification and exclusion frequently manifest within targeted marketing campaigns, as underscored by Jörg Scheffer. For readers seeking to dig deeper, *Platform Urbanism* by Sarah Barnes, another instalment of our "Geographies of Media" series, provides an enriched discourse on the subject matter. While personalisation of product information and shopping incentives may benefit certain consumers, the wholesale curation of news is inherently less benign. The drive toward crafting the most individualised milieu within the realm of social media juxtaposes with the targeted dispensation of news and information, yielding a profoundly disruptive force upon societal dynamics. *Mirrored Spaces* incisively demonstrates that circumscribed exposure to a constellation of perspectives potentially impedes the cultivation of diverse literacy and critical cogitation. The "filter bubble" emerges to expound upon the existence of "social divides in cyberspace as well as in real space". Our perception of the internet must evolve beyond a mere educational and sociocultural instrument to encompass a dynamic environment wherein economic interests and private agendas inexorably engender partial and non-neutral experiences. A determined examination is thus imperative.

Or, as Ricky Gervais puts it: "I think it's important to hold a mirror up to society and yourself".

Erfurt, Germany Torsten Wissmann
Quezon, Philippines Joseph Palis

References

Barns, S. (2020). Platform urbanism. Negotiating platform ecosystems in connected cities. Palgrave Macmillan.

Boos, T. (2017). Inhabiting Cyberspace and emerging cyberplaces. The case of Siena, Italy. Palgrave Macmillan.

Praise for *Mirrored Spaces*

"Examining digitalisation – in its multiple forms and social implications – from a spatial science perspective is a formidable challenge that the author takes on with great expertise and thoroughness. He memorably and convincingly illustrates how social inequality is reproduced under the influence of the data economy through unequal allocations of information and services that actually serve as resources for capital accumulation."
—Prof. Dr. Jürgen Rauh, *University of Würzburg, Germany*

"This book makes a key contribution to a deeper understanding of a core challenge of our time: the fact that despite enduring narratives of digital empowerment, the benefits of digitalisation remain unequally socially distributed. The author explains how individual socialisation conditions impact digital empowerment, and how this results in an increasing social divide."
—Prof. Dr. Tabea Bork-Hüffer, *University of Innsbruck, Austria*

"Jörg Scheffer succeeds in illustrating the enormous importance that data plays in the reproduction of social structures today. He convincingly describes how socio-spatial inequalities can be further exacerbated in the process. His work brings an important contribution to the growing field of digital geographies by uncovering how new geographies are created by ongoing digital transformations."
—Prof. Dr. Georg Glasze, *FAU, University of Erlangen-Nürnberg, Germany*

About This Book

This study proposes a critical examination of the empowering potentials of digitalisation, relating it to every individual´s opportunity for social advancement. Does digitalisation in advanced service economies help to counter the growing polarisation between the rich and the poor?
  Numerous studies seem to indicate that digital technologies provide new access to information and knowledge, providing especially the disadvantaged with new possibilities of action in their daily lives. From a spatial point of view, the new digital options could overcome the confining structure of the conventional social space: Contact options are less restricted to one´s own environment, new ideas and role models reach beyond the physically close and resources from other places become available. The extent to which an individual´s socialisation can be determined by their physical environment is explained in detail with reference to Löw´s sociology of space, Bourdieu´s concept of habits and Hurrelmann´s theory of socialisation.
  Even though the different social spaces in increasingly segregated cities seem to indicate at first glance that digitalisation does create new opportunities, the thesis provides detailed evidence countering the hypothesis of social empowerment in the digital age. Referring again to Löw and Bourdieu, it reveals that the use of digital information is connected to highly one-sided socialisation influences which follow the economic rules of algorithms. Since virtually every internet activity is being recorded and converted into tailor-made, individualised offers, the virtual world

seems to conform more and more to every individual's characteristics. The oft-quoted filter bubble (Pariser) gains new relevance from a spatial perspective and in relation to opportunities for social advancement. Self-referential influences have a reverse-influence on action in physical and virtual social spaces and thereby tend to cement social differences.

The study substantiates these arguments through visualising district-related data through recorded consumption preferences, housing standards and income obtained from a major data dealer for the cities of Berlin, Munich and Essen. The maps show how different service providers confront individuals with their own characteristics on a daily basis, online as well as offline. The data referencing that results from this turns out to be more effective than the limitations of real space in the pre-digital age. Presently, people are more and more led into "mirrored spaces" which pre-select an individual's options of perception and actualisation, severely impeding opportunities for social advancement of disadvantaged social groups.

About the Author

Jörg Scheffer is Associate professor in Human Geography at the University of Passau. In 2019 he finished his habilitation in the field of cultural geography (Digitally Connected—Socially Divided. Inequality from a Spatial Perspective). His main research interests, in addition to digital geography and urban studies are in social and cultural geography.

Contents

1 **Introduction: Technological Competence and Social Change in a Spatial Perspective**   1
   References   6

2 **Stratification, Socialisation and Space**   9
  2.1 *Social Inequality in Post-industrial Society*   11
  2.2 *Approaches Following the Theory of Pierre Bourdieu*   15
  2.3 *Space in the Socialisation Process*   21
    2.3.1 *Segregated Social Spaces*   22
    2.3.2 *Social Inequality in Relational Space*   27
    2.3.3 *Neighbourhood and Site Effects*   32
    2.3.4 *Capital Locations and Their Selective Accessibility*   36
  2.4 *Interim Conclusion: The Spatial Deprivation of Opportunities*   43
  References   46

3 **Digital and Digitised Space as an Opportunity for Advancement**   53
  3.1 *Transformations into the Virtual: Structure and Plot*   56
  3.2 *Capital Acquisition in Cyberspace*   62
  3.3 *Digital Divides, Inequalities and Digital Habitus*   68
  3.4 *Interim Conclusion: The Digital Acquisition of Opportunities?*   72
  References   74

4 **Data-Based Utilisation Contexts**   79

4.1	Personalised Data and Their New Sources	81
4.2	An Efficient Form of Address: On the Utilisation of Personal Data	86
4.3	The Personalised Interaction Between Physical Space and Cyberspace	88
4.4	Mirrored Spaces	92
4.5	Interim Conclusion: Digital Self-Confrontation	98
	References	100
5	**Decontextualised Data and Socio-Spatial Differences**	**105**
5.1	Data as an Unequally Used Commodity	107
5.2	Data Traders and Their Portfolio	109
5.3	Empirical Findings in the Socially Segmented Urban Space	113
	5.3.1 Acquisition of Data and Procedure	114
	5.3.2 Berlin, Munich and Essen: Exemplary Attributions in Urban Space	116
	5.3.3 Externally Driven Site Effects	132
5.4	Interim Conclusion: Bourdieu in the Context of the Data Economy	134
	References	137
6	**Recursive Spaces—Conclusion and Outlook**	**139**
6.1	Ternary Recursivity	141
6.2	Outlook: Social Determination as an Overarching Challenge	147
	Bibliography	151

List of Figures

Fig. 5.1	Berlin—Lower class and instalment loans	118
Fig. 5.2	Berlin—Holders of academic degrees and business magazines	119
Fig. 5.3	Munich—Lower class and quality of residential location	123
Fig. 5.4	Munich, Ramersdorf-Perlach—Purchasing power index and concern for the environment	125
Fig. 5.5	Munich—Upper class and product novelty	126
Fig. 5.6	Munich—Product novelty and instalment loans in a comparison of neighbourhoods	128
Fig. 5.7	Essen—Upper class and quality of the residential area	130
Fig. 5.8	Essen—Lower class and TV shopping	131
Fig. 6.1	Types of recursive address (a–d)	144

CHAPTER 1

Introduction: Technological Competence and Social Change in a Spatial Perspective

Abstract Examining the entrenched inequality of opportunity between privileged and disadvantaged segments of society from the vantage point of digitalisation is a matter of urgency. The promise of individual technological empowerment should have an impact on the entire society and provide especially those who are disadvantaged with new opportunities. This guiding question will be elaborated on in the following, highlighting the special relevance of a spatial perspective. With a view on the chapters following, the subsequent approach will be laid out.

Keywords Digitalisation · Space · Internet · Opportunity · Social advancement

Where do you want to go today?

When Microsoft used this question in its image campaign in the mid-1990s, the technical possibilities of the emerging age of digitalisation were already looming on the horizon. The PC had become an established feature at desks all over the world and the internet was showing rapid growth rates. It could be utilised for the advertising promise of *technological empowerment* in a convincing way. Wherever users want to go, the software giant's promise went, its user-friendly technology provided the means.

A quarter of a century later, the big tech companies are no less ambitious. The telecommunications provider Cisco is picking up on the empowerment narrative with the slogan "The Bridge to possible", while Samsung, the world's largest producer of smartphones, is drawing attention to new options for action that are open to networked users in its "Do what you can't" campaign.

Together, they are pointing to a future full of possibilities that is already becoming evident in many ways. Smart cities dispose of automated ways to provide for their consumers, artificial intelligence liberates workers from more arduous types of labour and "omniscient" digital assistants follow our orders on demand. At the same time, driverless transport is becoming more and more normal, and with the help of our smartphones we can control and monitor networked objects. In light of these developments, individual opportunities seem to be multiplying: The promise of unrestricted mobility no longer refers only to the internet or the use of office applications, but it even affects the actions we perform offline. Smart services offer us the promise of taking over unpleasant activities, giving us more comfort, time and freedom.

Digital business models from online shopping and holiday bookings to telemedicine demonstrate the enormous potential of the digital economy's new service providers. Here, technological empowerment reveals itself in the ability to relocate entire value chains with the help of digital services. Even in traditional industries, efficiency and cost benefits from digitalisation are now so obvious that any clinging to familiar operating procedures proves problematic as soon as competitors are taking advantage of the new opportunities. More than ever, the ability to adapt quickly to innovations is a question of economic survival.

In light of these developments, policymakers are called upon to pave the way for digitalisation through successful funding policies, infrastructure and education measures, which is reflected in national and EU-wide initiatives as well as in the rhetoric of politicians. During the COVID-19 pandemic, digital service gained even more in importance in the public and private sectors alike. There are other major challenges that the digital transformation offers solutions for. Planners envision resource-efficient cities as an answer to the environmental crisis and offer intelligent control in the face of overburdened transport systems.

Another challenge is presented by the increasing social divide in numerous countries. Even in the more advanced economies whose populations enjoy a high level of prosperity on average, growing differences within societies cannot be denied. Numerous studies have identified a sharp rise in income polarisation and increasing wealth concentration caused by massive dislocation processes. They reveal inequality between rich and poor not only in terms of quality of life, opportunities of participation and realisation, but also in the limited options of disadvantaged segments of the population to modify social stratification, as resources to improve one's social position are also unequally distributed. Consequently, the different contexts of education and socialisation contribute to a perpetuation of inequality and polarisation in society thus turns into a structural problem.

Against the backdrop of entrenched inequality, digitalisation appears as an obvious solution. The promise of technological empowerment mentioned above should have an effect on society as a whole, offering new options to the disadvantaged segments of the population. If the reason business leaders and politicians demand a greater investment in digitalisation lies in the potential of the new technologies for society as a whole, this should also mean that it includes new opportunities for the disadvantaged segments of the population as well. The general promise of mobility behind slogans such as "Where do you want to go today?" or "Do what you can't" needs to be put to the test.

Today, smartphones are ubiquitous in all parts of society, and free apps and many other easily accessible services seem to offer new options for action. Potentially, they could spread resources relevant for advancement such as education, social contacts, ideas and life paths, counteracting structural inequality in a sustainable way. Based on these premises, the possible impact of the digital revolution on the social question needs to be explored.

Several studies from the fields of media pedagogy and education research are tying the acquisition of competencies and knowledge to the new offers from digital media. While they show that the empowerment hypothesis needs to be qualified to the extent that conditions for media acquisition and usage are not equal across society (digital divides), the opportunities created by digitalisation are also acknowledged (Glăveanu et al. 2020; Rienties et al. 2022). From the perspective of social theory, the widespread euphoria about the technical possibilities is countered with the unequal control over the technical infrastructure, which is always tied to the question of power. Moreover, sociologists of technology are pointing out that the digital technologies are increasingly acting autonomously, influencing the world around them (Airoldi 2022;

Rohlinger and Sobieraj 2022). Only certain actors can program them, a fact which brings social hierarchies back into the picture (i.e., Kitchin & Dodge 2011). The widespread discourse on surveillance also argues against the potential that digital technologies offer to users, viewing them as forms of control and discipline instead. With frequent reference to Michel Foucault's "Discipline and Punish" (1979), new technologies have been understood as a means of maintaining the existing order by subjecting every individual to a sense of permanent visibility (Klauser et al. 2014; Gabrys 2014).

Finally, the empowerment hypothesis can also be countered with the current discourse on privacy (Beyvers et al. 2017). The use of new technologies is here associated with the loss of the private sphere through the surrender of personal data. This leads to a transparency of each individual which has a far-reaching effect on the social regime by influencing power structures and inequalities that were tied to the practices of privacy.

Those who are more optimistic about the consequences of digitalisation could reply that many of these arguments tend to point out general challenges that disadvantaged segments of the population are not necessarily affected by. While it may be true that societies are changing because of digitalisation and that surveillance, control and loss of privacy are real issues, the opportunity for individual social mobility is also real (Ferger 2018; Daniela 2022).

The present study wants to contribute to this this contradictory debate about the social effects of digitalisation. However, it does so with a clear focus on individual socialisation conditions and opportunities for advancement as well as a related analysis of the conditions of technical empowerment in the context of a growing social divide.

Throughout, the question of digital empowerment will be explored from a spatial perspective. The central argument is that social disadvantage corresponds to spatial structures and that the entrenchment of social inequality can only be understood in a spatial context. Only by countering the unequal social conditions in physical real space with other conditions that claim to be more favourable for social advancement can the alleged possibilities of digitalisation be put to the test.

Based on current findings about the growing social divide in numerous societies, we will first look at its causes (Chapter 2.1–2.2). A broad concept of social inequality, going beyond wealth and income, reveals a fundamental inequality of opportunity between different segments of the population. Germany is used as an example to demonstrate how inequality results from different socialisation conditions and how these unequal conditions for obtaining education and work are in turn reproduced. Pierre Bourdieu's classic studies will be used for a more in-depth analysis of the mechanisms of social perpetuation.

In a spatial context, the unequal distribution of opportunities turns out to be even more restrictive (Chapter 2.3). The opportunity structure of each individual in the urban space is greatly determined by the neighbourhood. Resources for upward mobility, as differentiated in Bourdieu's various types of capital, are unequally divided in space and because of mechanisms of distinction and differentiation, they are also unequally accessible. If we assume that spaces and spatial conditions are created on a daily basis, as done by Martina Löw in her relational concept of space, a further kind of resource-dependent inequality becomes evident: Socialisation and opportunities for advancement are regimented on a spatial level as capital-strong actors can obtain more favourable conditions than capital-poor ones.

Based on these social and spatial mechanisms of perpetuation, Chapter 3 will ask how digitalisation can be used to help disadvantaged segments of the population. The parallel world created by cyberspace calls for a reflection on how its structures and opportunities for action differ from real space and under what conditions an acquisition of capital can facilitate social advancement. Chapter 4 will enhance the debate over social empowerment through digital technologies with a look at the costs. Users of digital technologies pay for them with personal data. These are then tied to products, information and services and sent back to the users. While many other studies focus on (governmental) surveillance or the loss of privacy, the leitmotif of the present investigation is the importance of self-mirroring through the data economy. What are the social implications of user targeting when this means an economic translation of the user's own dispositions?

Further exploring the possibilities of a recursive acquisition, Chapter 5 takes us back to the neighbourhood. Based on commercially traded data, individual German cities will be used as examples to ask in what way a data-based exploitation logic reaches the neighbourhoods and their residents and what this implies for socialisation and the social question in general. Finally, Chapter 6 will summarise the findings and connect them again to the hypothesis of digital empowerment. What is apparent for the digital age is an economically defined opportunity structure which transmits social opportunities in a highly unequal way, thereby shedding a new light on the social question. In the interpenetration of the physical and virtual space, the new networking technologies have a structuring power that remains hidden behind the technological promise of slogans like "Do what you can't".

Step by step, this study will reveal that in our digitalised present, the social stratification processes in fact have to be looked at in a different way, albeit not in the sense of technological empowerment. What a spatial perspective actually reveals is that the socially disadvantaged segments of the population are confronted with new reproductive mechanisms that solidify the status quo and cement social differences. Surprisingly, the more the digital offers are used, the likelier this is.

References

Airoldi, Massimo (2022): *Machine Habitus: Toward a Sociology of Algorithms*. Cambridge: Polity.
Beyvers, Eva; Helm, Paula; Hennig, Martin; Keckeis, Carmen; Innokentij, Kreknin & Püschel, Florian (eds.) (2017): *Räume und Kulturen des Privaten*. Wiesbaden: Springer VS.
Daniela, Linda (ed.) (2022): *Inclusive Digital Education*. Cham: Springer.
Ferger, Edwin (2018): Anwendungen der Informations- und Kommunikationstechnologie und die Mediatisierung sozialer Inklusion. In: Aljoscha Burchardt & Hans Uszkoreit (eds.): *IT für soziale Inklusion*. Berlin, Boston: De Gruyter, 69–76.
Foucault, Michel (1979): *Discipline and Punish: The Birth of the Prison*. Alexandria: Alexander Street Press.
Gabrys, Jennifer (2014): Programming Environments: Environmentality and Citizen Sensing in the Smart City. *Environment and Planning D* 32 (1), 30–48.
Glăveanu, Vlad; Ness, Ingunn & Saint Laurent, Constance de (eds.) (2020): *Creative Learning in Digital and Virtual Environments: Opportunities and Challenges of Technology-Enabled Learning and Creativity*. New York: Routledge.
Kitchin, Rob & Dodge, Martin (2011): *Code/Space: Software and Everyday Life*. Cambridge: MIT Press.
Klauser, Francisco; Paasche, Till & Söderström, Ola (2014): Michel Foucault and the Smart City: Power Dynamics Inherent in Contemporary Governing Through Code. *Environment and Planning D* 32 (5), 869–885.
Rienties, Bart C.; Hampel, Regine; Scanlon, Eileen & Whitelock, Denise (eds.) (2022): *Open World Learning: Research, Innovation and the Challenges of High-Quality Education*. London: Routledge.

Rohlinger, Deana A. & Sobieraj, Sarah (2022): *The Oxford Handbook of Digital Media Sociology*. New York: Oxford University Press.

Open Access This chapter is licensed under the terms of the Creative Commons Attribution 4.0 International License (http://creativecommons.org/licenses/by/4.0/), which permits use, sharing, adaptation, distribution and reproduction in any medium or format, as long as you give appropriate credit to the original author(s) and the source, provide a link to the Creative Commons license and indicate if changes were made.

The images or other third party material in this chapter are included in the chapter's Creative Commons license, unless indicated otherwise in a credit line to the material. If material is not included in the chapter's Creative Commons license and your intended use is not permitted by statutory regulation or exceeds the permitted use, you will need to obtain permission directly from the copyright holder.

CHAPTER 2

Stratification, Socialisation and Space

Abstract The social upheavals happening in Western countries through a drifting apart of society—creating a wealthy minority on the one hand and increasing insecurity on the other—carry a great potential for conflict especially when they seem to become structurally entrenched. Starting with the development and the causes of social inequality today, the process of social reproduction needs to be examined closely, the goal being a step-by-step comprehension of upward mobility in the internet age. To this end, the acquisition of knowledge and qualification (according to Pierre Bourdieu and Martina Löw, among others) must be put in the larger context of socialisation and its spatial contingency in order to be able to identify group-specific mechanisms of privilege and discrimination more thoroughly.

Keywords Social advancement · Socialisation · Bourdieu · Site effects · Cultural capital · Relational space

Despite its continuing relevance, the classic topic of social inequality between and within societies has gone through different phases over the decades in terms of the attention it has received, influencing public discourse in different ways. The question of what constitutes inequality is, by its nature, normative and charged with value. It depends on what is considered valuable and desirable within a society and to what extent corresponding goods and services are attainable for the individual. The limited nature of material wealth, power or prestige and the selective accessibility of resources lead to differences in distribution, whose meaning must always be defined and negotiated in the socio-political context. Different viewpoints notwithstanding, in general the acceptance of social stratification seems to be decreasing when individual options for action are restricted to such an extent that an improvement of one's social position is hardly possible. In the recent past, more and more findings have corroborated this development. Not only is it clear that income and wealth are becoming more and more polarised in the wealthiest countries, but also that the losers are permanently forfeiting essential opportunities, passing this burden on to their children. In addition to the distribution of economic resources, socialisation and educational contexts contribute to a class-related segregation that greatly limits social advancement.

The current revival of the debate on inequality draws important arguments from this logic of reproduction. Adding further relevance to it is the fact that in the post-Fordist economies, many occupations are now being lost that used to secure resources and a sense of belonging for workers. The emerging digital age is accompanied by completely new skills requirements. Education will become even more important, and with it the question of accessibility. If digital technologies such as the smartphone are also seen as new tools for acquiring knowledge and qualifications, there seems to be no quick answer to the question of which groups will emerge as the loser from the process of change on the labour market. In fact, some researchers in the field of education argue that this transformation could uncover hitherto unknown access to resources, to the benefit of those who were disadvantaged in a reproductive distribution system.

To assess the opportunities for advancement in the internet age, the process of social reproduction has to be discussed in more detail, with the development and causes of social inequality in the present as the point of departure. In order to identify group-specific mechanisms of advantage and disadvantage more comprehensively, the acquisition of knowledge and qualifications must be placed in the broader context of socialisation and its spatial conditionality.

2.1 Social Inequality in Post-industrial Society

Characterising the present as a time of dramatic changes in the labour market, a dismantling of the welfare state and a dramatic increase in inequality of life chances also means comparing it to a past that was characterised by a high degree of social convergence. This is true for the Fordist post-war era of the 1950s and, in particular, the 1960s in Western Europe and the United States. Since the demise of this era in the 1970s, the debate over the social question, especially related to inequality of income, has again become relevant as the "new social question". Presently, there is even talk of a dramatic regression, with parallels to the class divide of the nineteenth century in terms of inequality and life chances (Siebel 2012, p. 472).

While wages in the simple service sector are lagging behind overall income development, they are currently growing in the field of high-productivity (high-value) services. On the one hand, a growing number of unemployed or low-skilled workers, single parents or older people have difficulty coping with the demands of the modern labour market (Schürz 2016), while on the other hand the winners of modernisation benefit disproportionately. Over the years, high-income earners have been able to use their powerful positions to increase their income, even though the relative level compared to low incomes does not correspond to the respective productivity (Piketty 2014). Growing income inequality is evident in longitudinal studies for almost all highly developed service nations (Atkinson et al. 2011; Rohrbach 2008, p. 195ff; United Nations 2020; Kakwani 2022). A common finding is that the shares of households in the middle income groups are decreasing, while those in the upper and lower-income groups are clearly increasing. If we focus on the wealth situation of households, the contrasts that have emerged in recent decades become even sharper. In Europe alone, which still has the smallest contrasts in a continental comparison, there have been strong polarisations over the last few years: The Top 10% in Europe captures 58% of total household wealth, versus 38% for the Middle 40% and 4% for the Bottom 50% (Chancel et al. 2022). Within the country groups, the differences are sometimes even more drastic. In Germany, for example, the richest ten per cent of the population own more than 67% of total net wealth. For the richest one per cent it is over 35%, and for the richest one per thousand it is still 20% (Deutsche Bundesbank 2022).

The extreme inequality of wealth produces contrasting life realities of privilege and complete deprivation, which are not only evident in quality of life, opportunities of participation and realisation, but can also mean a difference in life expectancy of up to 10 years (Lampert and Rosenbrock 2017).

Among the numerous explanations for the extreme accumulation of wealth among the propertied classes is the productivity of capital, whose income generally grows faster in percentage terms than the economy as a whole (Piketty and Saez 2006). Other reasons are the options of tax reduction or evasion (tax havens) (Druyen et al. 2009), or the increasingly unequal distribution of inherited income (Frick and Grabka 2009).

Yet, the most important explanation of social polarisation processes concerns the question of income generation and its preconditions. Economic and sociological studies point in two directions here: Among economists, the thesis of skill-biased technological change can be found frequently, which sees the increasing importance of relevant qualifications as the main reason for rising income inequality. Against the backdrop of technological change, especially in connection with the spread of modern computers, the demand for highly qualified workers is rising sharply. As has been widely demonstrated in the early stages of computer diffusion in the United States, this leads to substantial wage gaps between skilled and unskilled workers, which are increasing over time (Bound and Johnson 1992; Levy and Murnane 1992; Autor et al. 1999, among others). The outlined polarisations within the growing service spectrum between unskilled labour and highly specialised activities fit into this diagnosis. The emerging integration of industrial production with modern information and communication technology ("Industry 4.0") will give further impetus to the polarisation processes, as highly paid services continue to displace industrial activities. Further ahead, scholars are predicting the emergence of a global precariat in a fully connected world, when it will be possible to distribute most digital services under global competition on increasingly poor terms (Graham and Anwar 2019).

To counter this economic explanation of income inequality as a function of supply and demand, sociologists use closure theory (for an overview, see Mackert 2004). According to this, elites manage to secure increasing incomes for themselves and exclude others from professional fields of activity and the wealth gains of the national economy through discrimination mechanisms, processes of distinction, institutional changes and class conflicts. From this perspective, privilege through citizenship can be as much a restriction on competition as the requirement of degrees for certain professions.

Both approaches focus on the lack of social mobility of low-income earners, which, according to the concept of skill-biased technological change, is also based on the need for education and qualifications. This raises the question of equal opportunity with regard to individual education. In many OECD countries, the educational path taken greatly depends on the income and qualifications of the parents, resulting in the reproduction of social inequality. Children from lower-status backgrounds are demonstrably less likely to acquire a higher educational qualification than children from higher-status backgrounds. Further limits to social mobility are set by the difficulties to enter the education market or a certain educational institution faced by older people, single parents or immigrants.

Closure theory views social mobility as regulated from the outside, which highlights the importance of the exclusion mechanisms that are already taking effect in the education process. While a lack of education and training certificates itself acts as a closure mechanism, other mechanisms of empowerment or restriction, which have to do with social background, milieu, place of residence and other socialisation conditions, are at play even before. From this perspective, too, an inequality of opportunity with self-reinforcing effects can be observed: While the "inside" creates a sense of belonging and guarantees access to resources relevant for advancement that consolidate the status achieved, the "outside" deprives the individual of the necessary access, cements or diminishes the existing position and puts them at a relative disadvantage in the competition with others. Therefore, for the study of social polarisation it makes sense to first look at the fields of opportunity and access to resources that individuals and groups dispose of.

The ability to individually improve one's social position depends not only on personal preconditions but also on living conditions. These are usually divided into the categories of differences in education, gainful employment, wealth, power, prestige, as well as different working, living and leisure conditions (cf. also Rössel 2009). Education is at the centre of this web of enablers and constraints. Its paramount importance is reflected in countless publications that analyse it in the context of changing occupational demands or—more generally—conceptualise it as the most important enabler of social participation (Miethe et al. 2017; Piketty 2014; Castells 2009; chapter 4). It is to be understood here in both respects—as a never-ending process that facilitates the development of an independent personality capable of solving problems and mastering life, and therefore having a very fundamental effect on the individual's options for action.

Yet viewing education as a central prerequisite for professional and social success should not make us forget that education systems are only one aspect of a comprehensive socialisation process whose complex components are made up of individual psychological and external social conditions. The individual's chances of succeeding in the labour market through education and knowledge are thus dependent both on personality formation and development and on the social and material environment mediated by society. With their model of productive processing of reality, Hurrelmann and Bauer (2018) have placed socialisation in this double context of internal and external reality. Accordingly, personality development is conceived as a constant interaction of individual development and the surrounding factors. "Whether or not the individual is successful in coping with these tasks depends on the personal and social resources available to him or her. The demand to balance personal individualisation and social integration in order to safeguard self-identity is present in all phases of life and development" (Hurrelmann and Bauer 2018, p. 23). The authors divide the socio-spatial conditions into contextual factors, which concern the material equipment, the symbolic occupation as well as the standardisation of a surrounding space, and into compositional factors. The latter denote the composition of the group to which people belong or in which they act.

While education and the acquisition of knowledge in the socialisation process thus generally hold the promise of social participation, this promise depends on equal opportunities in the acquisition of education. Tracing the life course of the individual, which takes place in stages from the early years, through young adulthood, middle adulthood to older and oldest adulthood, reveals that the living conditions, or—in terms of socialisation theory—the contextual and compositional factors in these stages differ considerably between rich and poor.

Serious social inequalities can be documented for all phases of life, which in turn contribute to the inequalities in the socialisation process. A central part of this process is the ongoing internalisation of experiences, the aforementioned "productive processing of the internal and external reality" (Hurrelmann and Bauer 2018, p. 23), which ties back to the individual reservoir of action and perception, providing specific options.

Pierre Bourdieu's famous theory of class (especially 1984) offers itself as a starting point for a deeper examination of the different chances to reach upwardly relevant resources in physical real space and, on further consideration, in virtual space. It connects well with Hurrelmann's dualism of personality development and environmental influences: Bourdieu resolves the polarity between the objectivist and subjectivist position, between socially shaped and autonomously acting individuals via the habitus concept, which takes up the social structure and in turn structures people's thoughts and actions. The individual does not face his environment in isolation, but incorporates it and unites with it. Objective structures of living conditions—such as income or level of education—and subjective motives for action, dispositions and knowledge thus correspond to a high degree.

2.2 Approaches Following the Theory of Pierre Bourdieu

Bourdieu's theory of class has long been established in the fields of socialisation, education and stratification research, proving its theoretical adaptability and explanatory power until the present. Furthermore, it has provided an interdisciplinary reference point for a wide range of research interests. Depending on the approach, the French sociologist's extensive oeuvre is taken up as a model of lifestyles, theory of practice or habitus concept, all of which in no way denies the consistent design of the basic theoretical framework. The following summary of some of Bourdieu's central findings focuses on the relevance of his work for socialisation theory—mainly with reference to his most important study (Bourdieu 1979, 1984)—by addressing capital acquisition and intra-class habitus acquisition of reproductive patterns of disposition. In a further step, the relevance of the physical space can be connected to this, something which Bourdieu himself did only to a limited extent (Bourdieu 1991, 1999).

Bourdieu developed the concept of social space as a foundation for explaining economic-social conditions (classes) and lifestyles and how they mutually condition one another. He understands social space as a relational structure of social positions (not to be confused with places or territories in real space) whose coordinates reflect the positions of individuals and groups. On a first level, class-related positioning can be determined in this web of social relations. As is well known, Bourdieu defines this according to the capital endowment, which he detaches from a purely economic view, in contrast to the previous analysis of class: "The primary differences, those which distinguish the major classes of conditions of existence, derive from the overall volume of capital, understood as the set of actually usable resources and powers..." (Bourdieu 1984, S. 114). Besides economic capital, which is capital that can be converted into money (such as property and assets), Bourdieu refers here to social and cultural capital. *Cultural capital* can take on three forms, as (a) embodied, (b) objective and (c) institutionalised capital:

a. Embodied cultural capital refers to knowledge and education. In the broadest sense, education encompasses different capabilities and skills that individuals acquire in an ongoing socialisation process in the family, at school and in the social environment. This includes specialised knowledge in a field of science just as much as preferences in taste, personal appearance in the context of what is appropriate or individual speaking skills. These are acquired capabilities and skills that cannot be bought with money nor can they be inherited. At the same time, their incorporation is based on a class-based potential related to patterns of education, access to cultural incentives or social contacts in the neighbourhood. Thus the described perpetuation of the social class puts the focus on the incorporated capital through ongoing internalisation of the available educational offers and the reproduction of available resources. From the point of view of closure theory, the unequal opportunity to invest in education can be understood as a guarded advantage of the elites. They are the ones setting the rules that define which cultural norms are legitimate and which are not.
b. In addition to embodied capital, Bourdieu talks about objective capital, which includes cultural goods (e.g., books, paintings, instruments). Because of their materiality, they can be passed on as property. However, they are only useful as a strategically applicable form of capital if the actor is also aware of the importance of these goods and possesses the corresponding embodied capital.
c. Institutionalised capital refers to titles. The possession of titles (certificates, diplomas, academic degrees) certifies that an individual possesses specific cultural skills and abilities. Due to their institutional recognition, titles make a conversion into economic capital possible, such as when the successful completion of an educational programme is accepted as proof of qualification for entry into

the professional world. Institutionalised capital thus also exhibits interrelationships with Bourdieu's other types of capital mentioned, since the professional career is influenced both by embodied and economic (and also objectified) capital, and the acquisition of these capitals is in turn either favoured or made more difficult by the profession and income.

By *social capital*, Bourdieu understands a person's social network that they can fall back on. Friends, memberships or business contacts entail different group memberships that can help gain resources relevant for advancement, whether through an important information (e.g., about a job opening, a real estate property), preferential treatment (e.g., getting a job or a loan) or another form of help. Here again, the capital endowment greatly depends on the family of origin, even if effort to maintain the contacts is necessary. To acquire further social capital, the living environment needs to be considered, as the usual places a person frequents to a large extent predetermine with whom and under what circumstances contacts are possible in the first place.

Finally, Bourdieu introduces a further, overarching type of capital, which he termed *symbolic capital*. It refers to the prestige or reputation attributed to a person based on the three aforementioned types of capital, for example, because of contacts, titles, education or wealth.

To determine one's position in social space, the quantity and characteristics of the types of capital are decisive. While a cumulation of all types of capital might imply a clear social stratification, Bourdieu puts the emphasis on the construction of social classes resulting from the "relationships between all relevant characteristics" (1984, S. 114ff). In the coordinate system of economic and cultural capital, he locates individual professions and occupational groups that are endowed with specific capital. Thus, university lecturers, executives, doctors or entrepreneurs have a high volume of capital overall. Within this group, university lecturers have more cultural capital and entrepreneurs are characterised more by their economic capital. In comparison, semi-skilled workers or administrative employees, among others, are characterised by a low overall level of capital endowment. Bourdieu complements this space of objective class positions, which he calls the "space of social position", with the "space of lifestyles". Both are intimately connected to each other: Class is expressed in different lifestyles, such as how one dresses, one's taste in music or one's learning. In the coordinate system of capital endowment, clusters of specific tastes, preferences and activities are thus found that correspond to certain occupations: "Thus, grouped around the name of each class fraction are those features of its life-style which are the most pertinent because they are the most distinctive – though it may in fact share them with other groups" (Ibid., p. 131).

If a person's capital endowment correlates with their social position and manifests itself in certain lifestyles, then this presupposes class-specific structures of thought and behaviour. Bourdieu termed these "habitus". As a general attitude, as an internalised pattern of perception, thought and action, the habitus structures the world for the individual, determining what is acknowledged and approved of and what seems possible. As it develops over the course of socialisation, it is characterised by the class of origin and expresses an internalised social order: "This means that inevitably inscribed within the dispositions of the habitus is the whole structure of the system of conditions, as it presents itself in the experience of a life-condition occupying a particular position within that structure. The most fundamental oppositions in the structure (high/low, rich/poor etc.) tend to establish themselves as the fundamental structuring principles of practices and the perception of practices" (Ibid., S. 172). As the habitus has specific blueprints for processing reality built into it and the structure of reality is internalised as a meaningful order, social change becomes very difficult. While within one's own class, the habitus helps to meet the predominant codes and expectations, to create acceptance and belonging, it also limits the access to other classes. The internalised patterns of perception and judgement cannot connect to the conventions that exist there, or can only do so with difficulty. The reservoir of options for action, developed originally to protect oneself from experiences of crisis within the class, proves to be insufficient for entry into foreign classes and also inert for change (Bourdieu & Wacquant, 2013, S. 186f). For the lower classes, this means that they are denied access to types of capital which are relevant for upward mobility: They are deprived of certain contacts that could contribute to improving their position in terms of social capital. With regard to cultural capital, they remain unaware of the basis on which hiring and promotions take place regardless of professional qualification. They lack inspirations and role models to develop specific ambitions or to even be able to reflect on what the invisible rules of social advancement consist of.

In this process of social reproduction, numerous mechanisms of distinction are at work, through which classes distinguish themselves from one another on a symbolic level. Bourdieu contrasts the "taste for luxury" of the upper class with the "taste for necessity" of the lower class. The former defines cultural norms, seeking to distance itself from the masses through goods and styles whose value is based on rarity. Their habitus is expressed in their sense of taste, an affinity for the non-essential, a relaxed approach to rules and the will to secure their dominant position through social distinction. In his empirical studies on the "fine distinctions" in French society, most of which date from the second half of the 1960s, Bourdieu compiles a wide range of distinction practices. Overall, they reveal that "...there is no area of practice in which the aim of purifying, refining and sublimating primary needs and impulses cannot assert itself, no area in which the stylization of life, that is, the primacy of forms over functions, of manner over matter, does not produce the same effects" (Bourdieu 1984, p. 5). In nearly all areas of life, the economic class conflict is interwoven with a symbolic conflict over values and legitimate standards. The understanding of various codes, the correct implementation of rituals and a confident demeanour always presuppose, in addition to a lengthy process of understanding and internalisation, access to the class setting the standards. In the absence of this access, there is an inevitable lack of guidance and, more fundamentally, of class consciousness and understanding of the logic of stratification.

The competition among the ruling class for distinction on the one hand and the aspirations of the middle and lower classes on the other takes place in the various fields of culture, economy and politics. In the social struggle for prestige (symbolic capital), all types of capital are brought into play. According to Bourdieu, which capital combination prevails over the others always depends on the field. Its logic "...determines those which are valid in this market, which are pertinent and active in the game in question, and which, in the relationship with this field, function as specific capital- and, consequently, as a factor explaining practices" (Ibid., p. 113). The space of lifestyles with its power of distinction always has an effect on the space of social position, unleashing reproductive forces. From this perspective, a persistence of conditions of social inequality is not inevitable, but certainly probable.

In the interconnected world we live in today, however, there are additional options for action that the habitus concept cannot do justice to. It has been argued that social reproduction through the formative power of the habitus leaves the individual, embedded in social structures, with hardly any agency. Conditioned by one's class in a homogeneous and permanent manner, a person's possibility for self-development is so radically curtailed that it amounts to an external determination (e.g., DiMaggio 1979; King 2000).

In the 50 years that have passed since Bourdieu's empirical findings, the focus has shifted from the nation-state to an interconnected world. One could argue that individuals are today less determined by class, with educational and other options making completely new resources available, above all thanks to the internet. Whether the new possibilities in terms of information and communication can actually justify this expectation remains to be seen.

What must be said in defence of Bourdieu is that the reproducing power of the habitus by no means excludes deviating experiences and that variations are always possible through the individual habitus (e.g., Bourdieu 1984, p. 107f; Bourdieu and Wacquant 2013, p. 170). Nevertheless, collective influences appear to be sufficiently strong to allow capital-dependent differentiations to continue. More recent studies have, following Bourdieu, again identified classes in different countries and interpreted them with the help of the reproductive logic (e.g., Holt 1997 for the USA; Prieur et al. 2008 for Denmark; Bennett et al. 2009 for the UK). In addition, the clarity of reproductive mechanisms in the education system has been emphasised many times with reference to Bourdieu (Biermann 2009; Cushion and Jones 2012; Benson et al. 2015).

Without denying the serious inequality in many Western countries, we are undoubtedly witnessing an increase in opportunities for the individual compared to the past, which can be realised even with little economic capital. However, rather than proving Bourdieu's categories wrong, they reveal non-monetary structuring principles on a different level that are in line with the concept of the habitus. In today's world, where leisure activities and consumer goods that were once reserved to the upper class are available to everyone, differences in material wealth are much less decisive. Rather, knowledge of the upwardly relevant use of resources that precedes the consumption decision plays an essential role in explaining social differences. This knowledge in turn refers to the importance of Bourdieu's other types of capital and the difficulty of obtaining them. The question that must be asked is whether the conditions for such an acquisition have improved in recent years, particularly when they are examined in a spatial context.

2.3 Space in the Socialisation Process

The spatial environment, as a context of living and socialisation, has a significant influence on the opportunities of each individual. People who are born in the poor regions of the global South will generally find it harder to live in prosperity than those who grow up in economically and politically privileged environments. Growing up without the ability to satisfy basic needs will make it much more difficult to achieve a proper education, especially if the relevant institutions are not within reach or access to them is restricted. People who lack mobility and live on the periphery of countries with underdeveloped infrastructures are denied essential resources to improve their individual living conditions. Without a doubt, this unequal distribution of employment and educational opportunities of social security and statistically probable prosperity is particularly significant on a global scale. Even though the frame of reference of what is desirable within a given society does qualify the comparisons between the extreme differences on earth to a certain extent, a dramatic inequality of opportunity related to territory cannot be denied. In light of an increasingly globalised perception of "Western" lifestyles, those affected by this inequality are becoming more aware of it as a global form of injustice.

In the cities of developed service societies, unequal access to resources at the small-scale level can initially be conceptualised in a similar way. By correlating social stratification with specific urban neighbourhoods, residential and living spaces of varying quality can be identified. The use of remote educational institutions and recreational infrastructures or contact to other milieus can be complicated and expensive, which ultimately curtails the opportunities of many urban residents outside of their own neighbourhoods. According to Bourdieu, being confined to one's own neighbourhood also limits the chances of capital acquisition: Access to knowledge and educational institutions, to social and cultural capital, depend on one's location in the urban space.

At the same time, a structural perspective alone, conceptualising space as a container with embedded, unequally distributed resources, is insufficient as an explanation and interpretation of how social differences come into being. It implies a territorialisation of the social sphere where spaces and opportunity relations are fixed in a static and homogenising way. While this perspective highlights the spatial conditioning of action, it does not take into consideration that there already exists a plurality of perceptions and that spaces themselves are to be understood as acts of construction. A more expansive concept of space must also reflect the fact that these spatially unequal conditions of action are controlled from other places and by hidden actors.

Based on a rough differentiation between rich and poor in cities, the following section will therefore discuss a concept of space that—following Hurrelmann and Bourdieu—focuses on the duality of external, in part globally controlled conditions and individual possibilities, of structure and action. Martina Löw's relational concept of space is helpful in this context: Her sociology of space sees spatial structures as the result of actions on the one hand, while at the same time understanding them as an essential condition for the constitution of space. Partly drawing on Bourdieu, she formulates a broad conceptual framework that offers possibilities for understanding spaces as a (globally) manufactured and regulating structure in the process of social ascent. As a next step, Bourdieu's explanations on space as reproducing "site effects" will be addressed. Based on a synthesis of the theories of Löw and Bourdieu, taking into account their commonalities as well as their differences, the final aim will be a detailed presentation of the fundamental obstacles to the acquisition of capital in the context of a relational understanding of space.

2.3.1 Segregated Social Spaces

Several classic studies on the spatial distribution of population groups in urban space—including the Chicago School as well as Georg Simmel's urban sociology or Friedrich Engel's view of urban class society—have illustrated how urban populations worldwide can be differentiated according to various criteria such as lifestyle, age and social status. With these and other ways of distinguishing populations in urban space, the current discourse puts a strong emphasis on socio-economic fault lines: Socio-spatial polarisation processes in the major cities of Europe and the Western world find their current expression in terms such as "citadels for the rich", gated communities and privatised, exclusive spaces on the one hand, and islands of poverty, ghettos of social exclusion and a periphery of the "urban underclass" on the other. While talk of the "dual" or "divided city" may seem exaggerated with regard to wealthy countries, it does point to a development process explained above as a phenomenon of increasing inequality in the post-industrial age. The connection between social and spatial privilege (or lack thereof) can now be conceptualised in both directions: An individual's place of residence is primarily an expression of their available budget, their class and their individual dispositions. Conversely, a person's place of residence has a strong influence on their opportunities and social advancement. While socialisation plays a major role in the search for the preferred object as a filter of what is desirable and feasible and as the result of options for action, the chosen residential location and form of housing, for their part, provide contextual and compositional factors that have a strong influence on socialisation. With reference to Bourdieu's types of capital, it is thus a question, on the one hand, of their use for the individual realisation of the residential function and, on the other hand, of the opportunities for appropriating capital in the context of a given residential location.

In recent years, findings on socio-spatial polarisation, segregation and exclusion tendencies have gained additional significance (OECD 2018, p. 20ff.; Cucca and Ranci 2017; De Maio and Benjamins 2021). On the one hand, current processes of economic division, described above as a consequence of unequal opportunities of participation, employment and other means of acquisition (including inheritance), can directly be applied to the urban space, where the different means available to the population dictate the residential function depending on the neighbourhood. In addition to economic capital, however, academic degrees, positions and social contacts can also influence an individual's choices regarding housing type and location. Temporary employment or even unemployment, lack of assistance from third parties, lack of references or the inability to make a convincing presentation at the first contact interview can highlight the additional relevance of cultural and social capital.

On the other hand, the conditions of the post-Fordist transformation process itself must be related to cities and placed in the context of globalisation. Global capitalism creates a situation of intense competition between all locations below the nation-state level, especially cities as centres of economic activity. While it has already been addressed how economic deregulation and flexibilisation and the structural change caused by them impact employment and social security systems, the capacity for successful transformation has a strong influence on the urban system itself. Traditional locations of industrial production, which are losing jobs, inhabitants and attractiveness due to a lack of competitiveness, exist side-by-side with prospering production and service regions with high population growth. The economic status of a city is reflected in its population structure as well as its employment and wealth situation and, importantly, determines the real estate market. Here, the bet on rising returns is also taking place in a global arena, with international investors looking to commercialise the urban space. In recent years, privatisation, rezoning and modernisation have led to a new wave of gentrification, amounting to an income-based division of the population. In an attempt to counter the displacement of lower-income segments of the population, municipal representatives criticise the sale of social housing to private investors, more or less successfully seeking to create affordable housing in the face of budget consolidation and a growing influx of new inhabitants. They find themselves in a heated market environment that has given a strong boost to real estate prices thanks to a long-standing policy of low interest rates. Not surprisingly, residential segregation is particularly advanced in high-demand metropolitan areas (Musterd et al. 2017; Haandrikman et al. 2023).

In a functional sense as well, places with high-quality services, with control and management functions, produce a coexistence of rich and poor. Sassen (1994, 2001) has demonstrated in her well-known studies that social polarisation is structurally inherent in cities where globally operating companies have their headquarters. Attached to high-paying jobs in the corporate headquarters of finance, law or high-tech companies are always fields of activity supporting these processes with more basic services. Catering, cleaning or transportation are just a few areas of a low-wage sector that are indispensable for the functioning of global cities. Consequently, high-income earners exist side by side with low-income earners, which the cityscape reflects in the dualism of very different residential locations and an equally polarised demand for leisure facilities—from golf courses to gambling halls, fancy boutiques to mass merchandisers, luxury restaurants to fast-food chains. This shaping of space driven from the outside, resulting from international capital flows, global location decisions and related demand structures is displacing the traditional and once-stable connections between local employer and wage-dependent residential location. At a global level, market-based patterns of usage are being established, which affect the supply of labour locally and at the same time have an impact on the individual availability of space. As a result, the development of rents and land prices no longer lies solely in the hands of the municipality concerned. International investors are redefining the relationship between public and private space across large distances, and mobile populations, telematics and deindustrialisation are creating new spatial arrangements. As is becoming more and more evident, digitalisation leads to significant workspace shifts from the periphery to metropolitan centres with specific urban focal points where skilled employees in creative professions find the best location conditions for the emerging new economy (Florida et al. 2017). Increasingly, social spaces are the result of a complex interplay of a wide variety of factors that make up the attractiveness of a location in the post-industrial age.

Furthermore, in the context of unbounded competition, cities increasingly define their attractiveness beyond the realm of traditional location policy. This entails image campaigns, attempts to exploit future-oriented themes and stressing one's uniqueness. What newly created landmarks, ambitious revitalisation measures, the upgrading of the waterfront and costly cultural projects have in common is that they usually require private capital, with the commercial aspect always playing a role. At the same time, they fulfil their significance best in a central location. In this way, they make a city shine in places where capital is already concentrated or where the investors would like to see it spread (with a gentrifying effect). While urban planners in Europe and the United States have made attempts at constructional improvements in structurally weak urban areas, none of their measures have made a real difference when it comes to levelling the contrast between the wealthy centres and the potentially poor periphery. Although urban development in Europe and the United States can point to various constructional upgrading efforts in structurally weak urban areas, the examples are hardly conducive to fundamentally breaking up the contrast between prosperous centre and partially poor periphery. In many cases, the successful transformation of a disadvantaged neighbourhood through building and infrastructural measures has been achieved at the price of rising rents. It confronts the established residents with a desirable living environment and new jobs which they themselves cannot take advantage of due to a lack of qualifications and income. Sooner or later they are displaced, which reorganises the city's social structure without achieving a spatial reconciliation of social contrasts (Altrock and Kunze 2017; Dangschat 2017). The result is a solidification of a population distribution in the urban area that, for all the diversity of cities, nevertheless reveals social clusters and rough patterns. Castel formulates a tripartite division of society, dividing it into "zones of integration, vulnerability, and exclusion". Applied to concrete cities, these zones are empirically proven to have different spatial layouts and distributions across the urban space (for an overview, see Gornig and Goebel 2013, p. 57ff). The zone of integration comprises neighbourhoods with a population that is largely secure economically and well-connected within its milieu. The zone of vulnerability, on the other hand, concentrates neighbourhood residents whose employment security (and other economic security) is no longer guaranteed in the long run (Castel 2000). Siebel (2012, p. 467), referring to Castel, describes it as an extremely heterogeneous zone with a growing number of single-person households, a large number of atypically employed people and people in situations of transition. It is characterised by high fluctuation and acts as a catch-all for the urban population spectrum. The zone of vulnerability comprises people who, thanks to their cultural and social capital, are able to move up into the zone of integration, as well as those in living situations that are threatened by relegation. Thirdly, the zone of exclusion concentrates those urban residents who are in most cases permanently excluded from gainful employment or who are, at best, sporadically employed in low-paid jobs. Social contacts are few and predominantly with people from their own class. Of course every city is different and factors such as political influence, cultural conditions, topography, the housing layout depending on the size of the living units, inner-city abandonments or a specific location or traffic situation have to be taken into account, yet the growing social segmentation in urban space remains an undeniable fact (Kronauer and Siebel 2013; Quillian and Lagrange 2016).

According to this characterisation, the segmented city, as a solidified spatial distribution of types of use and populations, evokes various associations with the prevailing spatial environments: Visually appealing, well-kept, with lots of green spaces on the one hand, and a concreted, highly condensed and unsettled environment on the other. While such contrasts imply advantages and disadvantages in the everyday life of the inhabitants related to a different quality of life, their significance for an individual's opportunities of advancement goes even deeper. Beyond differences related to the aesthetic quality of buildings or everyday life, it is necessary to analyse the quality of the (urban) living and socialisation context and their reproductive effect, either in an enabling or restricting manner. The structures that create different conditions for individuals or, more generally, for milieus, must be related to the respective options for action. Understanding these urban structures also includes the question of their constitution in an interconnected world.

2.3.2 Social Inequality in Relational Space

Cities are not the result of a natural evolution, but of decisions. The unequal distribution of population groups in (urban) space has been presented as a resource-dependent process. In the competition for space, a market economy will see financially strong actors prevailing over financially weak ones, while the government provides a framework through laws, guiding principles and concepts of development. Physical structures that emerge in a city—such as the building of houses, the setting up of apartments, stores and offices, the demand for infrastructure and the use of leisure opportunities—are the result of actions in space. Furthermore, cities are the result of the power and capital resources available to each and the ability to not only occupy a specific place (e.g., as a homeowner or business owner), but also to shape it. Those who can use their social capital to exert influence in the city administration, who know someone who provides them with critical information, or who have a decisive influence on the design of a business district due to their economic capital, can more easily change the structures of a city than those who have very little power to influence the development of these structures. They have to find housing in the niches left over by the market or settle for low-paid jobs that leave them with fewer opportunities for participation and design. However, in order to understand the city as an allocation system of different opportunities (Häußermann and Siebel 2004, p. 117), it is essential to exert some influence over the potentials and to bring together the conditions that determine the possibilities of influence, thereby relating action and structure to each other. As will be shown, it is particularly via space that this process of relating becomes plausible: As a condition of action as well as an outcome thereof, it is crucial for the explanation of social differences and their reproduction.

In sociology, Martina Löw (2016, originally published in German in 2001) has elaborated a sociology of space; the main features of which will be considered in more detail below. Löw understands space as "a relational arrangement of social goods and people (living beings) at places" (Ibid., p. 188). Löw's central concept of arrangement (*[An]Ordnung*), simultaneously emphasises "order" (*Ordnung*) as a structural dimension as well as the process of putting in place (*Anordnen*), representing the dimension of action. It is social actors who carry out this arrangement, and their possibilities for action essentially depend on which material and symbolic factors they are confronted with and which resources for action are available. Löw distinguishes two processes involved in the constitution of space: "spacing" and "operation of synthesis". Spacing refers to the act of placing social goods and people as well as symbolic markers in certain locations. Common examples would be the construction of houses, the design of interiors or the surveying of boundaries. Every individual's act of synthesis taking place simultaneously makes it possible that goods and people can be related to each other and combined into spaces. This happens through processes of perception, imagination or memory (Ibid., p. 134ff). The multiple individual spatial references that now become possible are limited by routines in Löw's sociology of space. In line with Giddens and Bourdieu, Löw points out that routines reproduce social institutions and habitualise a person's actions. The habitual repetition of everyday actions results in a recursive reproduction of social structures. Similarly, routines and institutions result in spaces that can be described above the individual level and are generally accepted, ensuring regulated cooperation between people. Thus, a city consists of relatively stable and functionally directive spaces both externally (e.g., traffic areas, stores, cemeteries) and internally (e.g., theatre halls, restrooms, dressing rooms), described by Löw as "institutionalized spaces". They are those spaces "in which the arrangement has effect beyond one' s own action and results in conventional operations of synthesis and spacing. As an institutionalized arrangement, space becomes an objectivation, which means that it is experienced as objective though it is a product of human activity" (Ibid., p. 139).

Löw understands "spatial structures" as part of the social structure, existing side by side with other structures (political, economic, legal). Picking up on Giddens' (1984) definition of structure, arrangements of people and social goods into spaces are called spatial structures if they are codified in rules or secured by resources and recursively stored in institutions independent of place and time (Ibid., p. 145, p. 190). While rules serve to establish meaning and sanctions, resources address means of power. Institutions are permanent regularities of social action. They can refer to behaviour, conventions or the enforcement of rules. The process of constituting spatial structures is recursive because they are continually recreated from underlying rules and resources. With these components, Löw assigns a socially produced efficacy to the concept of spatial structures that implies further consolidation, without ever ruling out the possibility of creeping or radical change. Löw turns Giddens' "duality of structure" into a "duality of space": Spatial structures are produced by action and have an effect on action; they enable action and restrict possibilities of action.

In order to illustrate the mechanisms of social segregation in Löw's sense as an interplay of space and society, we will consider a fictitious, centrally located square in the centre of a city as an example. As an institutionalised space, this square offers various uses to the urban population (e.g., as a meeting place and place of exchange), the realisation of which (through demand, mode of use and constant designation) again reproduces the spatial structure of the square. For decades, all parts of society across all milieus frequented this square, ideally giving it the function of an agora. One day, however, the redesign of the square by a municipal authority ("spacing" as a structural upgrade) results in the decrease of the square's attractiveness for the lower classes, as the changed look results in processes of alienation and a gradual change in the user structure sets in. The effect of the spatial structure now undergoes a profound change: As the preferred meeting place of the predominantly affluent urban population, the purpose of the square changes and is updated on a daily basis by certain groups and milieus using it (and by the absence of lower-status segments of the population). While the continuity of the new spatial structure is guaranteed in the longer term also by the resources of its new users and, moreover, follow-up investments by the private sector in the vicinity of the square take effect, the options for action of the former visitors are severely limited. To them, this square as a place of exchange, information and capital acquisition is lost, even in the absence of any physical barriers. Due to the lack of social connection points and the changes in what is offered, continued use is no longer an option for them. The newly created space now pre-structures the actions of its visitors in a different way, the altered composition of the square's users taking on a fundamental significance.

This example could be carried even further, as in a gentrification process of entire neighbourhoods undertaken by private actors, a "spacing" that directly removes the power of disposal over a place from those affected by physical barriers, and the coupling of spatial with new legal structures (privatisation of public spaces). In any case, it is clear conceptually that the perspective adopted by Löw and the analytical tools she uses bring the social relevance of space into focus. To clarify the meaning of spaces even further, Löw also focuses on their symbolism (Ibid., p. 161ff) as well as processes of perception and the effects of atmospheres (Ibid.,

p. 171ff). In line with the overall relational approach, these dimensions are also relevant as a condition and a result of individual action. They impact categories of belonging and foreignness, create closeness and distance, can empower and inhibit and feed into processes of distinction. With reference to the above example, the social rededication of the square will become more intense and permanent to the extent that these invisible spatial references support collective demarcations.

Central ideas found in Bourdieu's logic of reproduction as described above fit well into Löw's relational concept of space and are partly taken up by her: The availability of social, economic and cultural capital is essential to the process of arranging. The example of the urban square makes it clear that the change in the spatial structure was first initiated by the public sector with available resources and largely within the framework of the given material conditions. Already at this point the question could be asked to what extent the local decision-makers were influenced by representatives of the respective milieus and whether the intervention, declared to be in the general interest, did not originate from the specific ideal of a group that was able to take over the power of discourse and design due to its capital endowment. The subsequent transformation of the square is characterised by the dominance of a group with a specific capital endowment. Their distinction through all types of capital (expensive clothing, labels, the use of exclusive consumer articles, the form of communication, etc.) leaves the former visitors of the square with few options of access. At the same time, it allows the new users to assure themselves of their own milieu. It serves as a reservoir for further capital accumulation, in particular by initiating contacts within the milieu.

From the point of view of the displaced inhabitants, on the other hand, the square loses its significance. Beyond the altered arrangement, the once familiar social space has given way to an atmosphere consisting of different components of unfamiliarity affecting all the senses. The prevailing mode of communication or unfamiliar odours alone (e.g., through the use of perfume as a means of distinction) might be sufficient to cause effective distancing. Shunned by the lower classes, the square loses its function as a place of education and socialisation as well as of capital acquisition, and as a contact exchange across classes. For the displaced, the internalisation of its specific irrelevance and the retreat into contexts close to their own milieu lead to a loss of orientations and stimuli relevant for upward mobility. The square they once frequented on an almost daily basis might disappear completely from their radar, negatively affecting the possibility of constituting space there and beyond due to the loss of resources. Instead, they settle in the socially familiar contexts of the city (e.g., socially disadvantaged and peripheral neighbourhoods), which in turn promotes a constitution of space that has a reproducing effect on its residents. In areas with more options for design, as in the context of personal property, this constitution of space is an expression of a class-specific internalisation. This spatial structure can then be understood and appreciated in a rather class-specific way, without the recognition of status-unrelated groups.

The habitualisation of a specific spatial structure consequently regulates the possibilities of acquiring capital in various ways and reproduces the options for action in a class-specific way. Against this background, the examination of the individual potential for the constitution of space becomes extremely important. Those in need of access, however, lack resources and awareness, as habitus pre-structures the perception of spaces along with their opportunities and deprivations. In Löw's terms, habitus influences the "spacing" and the "operation of synthesis".

While instead of Bourdieu's forms of capital, she uses Kreckel's (1992) related dimensions, and Löw assigns a similarly central importance to space for capital acquisition (Löw 2016, p. 177ff). The reproductive power of habitus is central to her sociology of space, though instead of milieus she chooses gender and class (Ibid., p. 146ff, p. 159) as structural principles of a society. She repeatedly emphasises that social stratification processes are strongly influenced by spatial structures: "The reproduction of social inequality is systematically possible and does occur at every level of the constitution of space. Structural principles such as class and gender permeate all levels of constitution and are instrumental in establishing advantages and disadvantages, exclusion and inclusion" (Ibid., p. 177).

Conceptually, Löw's relational understanding of space helps comprehend how spaces as arrangements can multiply and also how they can be isolated or produced in the form of global networks. With reference to Sassen, she traces the constitution of global cities, a phenomenon which can only really be grasped in the context of a virtually supported linkage structure (Ibid., p. 82ff). At this point, however, it must be asked how this virtual part of space itself can be explained by processes of action. Löw does not clarify whether this process of constitution is also to be understood as structure-forming and structure-reproducing and how the online and offline (spatial) structures differ from each other. She is right in basing her relational argument in the virtual space, but fails to explore the complexity of virtual spatiality in the same way. Yet it is precisely virtual space that seems to empower action in an unimagined way and could thus remove the obstacles to acquiring capital in real space.

In order to pursue this perspective further, the reproducing spatial structures in real space must be put in more concrete terms and aligned with Bourdieu's logic of reproduction. Relating Bourdieu's and Löw's explanations on space, the goal is to compare the limiting structures of physical space with the opportunities of virtual space.

2.3.3 Neighbourhood and Site Effects

Understood relationally, space is an expression of spacing and operation of synthesis that exposes countless perspectives, which have not only favoured but probably also complicated Löw's reception. Space can be understood in different qualities, temporal permanence or size; it can exist abstractly, in concrete physical terms, in an overlapping or extremely volatile state. In order to identify basic patterns of spatial regimentation in the socialisation process, the following section will take a generalised look at the segregated urban space and how it favours certain groups while putting others at a disadvantage in different neighbourhoods. The different living conditions, considered above in general and more in detail following Löw, are expressed in neighbourhood or site effects (Bourdieu 1999). This is not to ignore individual perceptions and strategies of appropriation and action, but they are subordinated to a generalising description of the structure.

When inhabitants of a city choose a place of residence (based on the capital available), they become part of spatial structures which have a huge influence on the opportunities of capital acquisition, even more so than legal, economic or political structures. Unlike the public square described above, which is visited for a short time, the place of residence with its functions is a permanent point of reference in everyday life. Its significance as a context of socialisation goes far beyond the residential environment itself, as all activities are related to it in terms of the space of action and as a synthesis of the city. In terms of generally negative neighbourhood effects, there are direct disadvantages related to housing and its surroundings: Confined housing conditions, inadequate equipment or poor accessibility (Kronauer and Vogel 2004). In addition, disadvantaged urban neighbourhoods are characterised by neglected buildings, a negative appearance of the neighbourhood as well as infrastructural deficiencies, which includes the equipment of local places of encounter, green spaces or playgrounds and sports fields.

In this context of socialisation, the discrimination of neighbourhood residents already takes hold in childhood, when the physical environment is explored, and its relative deficiencies and shortcomings are internalised as normal and given. Lack of safety, confinement, decay and other manifestations of social inequality leave a mental imprint, shape the imagination and define individual possibilities. Since the family as the primary place of socialisation is also affected by the disadvantages of the neighbourhood, through its interaction it indirectly confronts the child with the environment and the consequences of its deficiencies (stress, fear, illness, deprivation) (Ecarius et al. 2011). In adolescence, the influence of the neighbourhood on its young population continues with lower-quality schools and peer groups possessing only those dispositions and visions that correspond to the familiar environment (Ainsworth 2002; Lauen 2016). Compared to privileged urban neighbourhoods, the awareness of one's status in a spatially disadvantaged context can negatively impact the self-image and perpetuate into adulthood. Recurrent feelings of exclusion are also a result of the physical environment of the neighbourhood and the living environment (Blasius et al. 2008, p. 112ff).

With the influence of neighbourhood residents on socialisation, the material dimension of detrimental neighbourhood effects gains a social dimension: In segregated neighbourhoods, social networks are largely homogeneous, which commonly inhibits the motivation to improve one's own situation. Children and adolescents seldom come into contact with social roles that represent alternative life paths beyond their own class. Instead, adolescents and young adults growing up in problem-ridden social contexts often strongly identify with the prevailing conditions. As a result, language and topics of interest, forms of recognition and life goals are established within the milieu and, over time, show fewer and fewer points of contact with the wealthier classes in other neighbourhoods. A partial exodus of the more capital-rich population segments that could offer incentives and other options contributes to a further homogenisation of the neighbourhood. Because of the architectural unattractiveness and the reputation related to the milieu, the influx from outside often remains limited to certain population groups. The effects of this symbolic discrimination are even more far-reaching by curtailing the opportunities for social participation of the residents.

Even before the lack of experience, conventions and contacts referred to above could come into play, decisions about who gets the job or the apprenticeship are often based on a person's place of origin and address.

Bourdieu relates neighbourhood effects to the social space described by him. While this is "...not the physical space, it tends to realise itself and in a more or less exact and complete way within it" (Bourdieu 1991, p. 28). Based on the unequal distribution of capital in society, he uses his own terminology to explain why certain privileged neighbourhoods enable further capital accumulation through "spatial profits", while disadvantaged neighbourhoods severely limit opportunities for capital acquisition and social advancement (Ibid., p. 31ff; 1999, p. 127f). Taken together, Bourdieu's examination of physical (urban) space as it is occupied by different milieus results in a hypothesis of perpetuation that attributes different "average probabilities" (Bourdieu 1991, p. 31) of further capital appropriation to the respective residential areas and that consolidates social difference on the basis of the mechanisms described. One of Bourdieu's main arguments for this perpetuation is the lack of knowledge of how to act adequately in spaces outside one's own class. As exemplified by the social reinterpretation of the central square, the physical accessibility of a place does not automatically include access to its resources. When someone lacks the education to successfully explore a museum, or the cultural capital to make contact in a distinguished residential area, it will be very difficult for them to acquire new cultural or social capital. Consequently, spatial convergence and social convergence do not automatically go together. "It is quite possible to physically occupy a residential area without actually and strictly residing in it; namely, if one does not have the tacitly required means to do so, beginning with a certain habitus" (Ibid.). When appropriation is not possible, people will ultimately stay away from areas outside of their own class, and in the long run this will have an influence on what they consider possible and desirable. Because of this field logic analysed by Bourdieu, people do not make use of what is outside of their milieu even when and if the ideal of a "social city" as devised by city planners and politicians, offering access to options for capital acquisition in different places, is realised. So, the same mechanism discussed above regarding educational systems is repeated here in real space.

This segmentation is further solidified by privileged residents sticking together, as they reassure each other of their capital resources and emphasise their separateness from those below them. Bourdieu uses the term "club effect" to describe these concentrations, caused in particular by economic and symbolic capital, "...of people and things that are similar in that they are different from the great mass, who have in common not to be common" (Ibid., p. 32). In contrast, the "ghetto effect" works against any advancement, as it collectively stigmatises neighbourhood residents, impeding advancement to other classes. Bourdieu uses exemplary urban spaces to stress this polarisation, referring to them as "posh neighbourhoods" or "luxury residential areas" on the one hand and "ghettos" or "a kind of reservation" for the poor on the other. Such contrasts can certainly be found in cities across Europe or North America, together with the manifestations of capital endowment: The successful lawyer living in an upper-middle-class *Gründerzeit* apartment furnished with works of art, who, in addition to the people in his neighbourhood, meets friends to visit classical concerts, gains distinction from the careful selection of his clothing and elite manners and who also maintains social distance in his practice of leisure sports and the choice of all his places of consumption. At a social and spatial distance from him, there is the single mother living in a large housing estate on the outskirts of the city. Due to insufficient income, her life focuses on the mere organisation and management of everyday life, and because of spatial, temporal, financial reasons as well as a difference in interests, there are no stimuli from outside her own class. This dualism makes the logic of a double (dis-)advantage particularly vivid, which, beyond the difference in the quality of life, highlights the unequal opportunity for capital acquisition available in the two spheres: The lawyer's milieu (as in the case of the rededicated square) offers him the possibility to expand his social network among professionals in higher positions, to update the relevant codes for upward mobility in all areas of life through everyday contact and, last but not least, to consolidate his position through economic capital. The single mother, on the other hand, finds herself in a living environment where social capital, education, taste and manners are passed on within the milieu, making it all but impossible to access resources relevant for advancement. However, such exemplary juxtapositions should not result in a reductionist understanding that relates the problem of social stratification only to extremes. Bourdieu himself repeatedly emphasised the hierarchisation of all fields of capital deployment and acquisition and the resulting hierarchisation of physical space, which objectifies and reproduces social space. "In the relationship between the distribution of actors and the distribution of goods in space, the respective value of the different regions of the reified social space is manifested" (Bourdieu 1999).

2.3.4 Capital Locations and Their Selective Accessibility

While Bourdieu's approach is useful for exploring social inequality as an interplay of social position, incorporation, lifestyle and corresponding spatial profits, the question remains—as mentioned in the introduction—whether his evaluation of physical space as reified social space is appropriate. In his discussion of Bourdieu, Schroer (2006, p. 100ff) suggests that social space does not necessarily have to fit into physical space. Not only does this result in questionable pre-categorizations by assuming an automatic connection between spatial phenomena and social conditions, but it also suggests a certain inertia with regard to social change. In the context of a stable urban arrangement, the persistence of physical space must ultimately negate existing processes of ascent and descent of individuals. Conversely, change in real space does not necessarily have to go hand in hand with social change. While social space as an expression of a capital-dependent struggle for position still functions in a relational perspective, its materialisation carries the danger of a reification of the social (cf. also Deffner and Haferburg 2012, p. 168). As a result, the social construction of spaces threatens to lose its meaning, and an alternative interpretation of existing spatial arrangements becomes impossible (Schroer 2006, p. 102).

A possible solution is offered by Löw's dualistic conception which understands space as a condition and consequence of its constitution. She conceptualises action as dependent on symbolic and material factors in each situation, which are themselves also the result of actions (Löw 2016, p. 161ff). When evaluating opportunities of capital acquisition, walls, distances or confined housing conditions undoubtedly constitute essential structures that must be factored into the analysis of possibilities for action, even if they themselves are also products that are multiplied in the context of individual dispositions. Coming back to the above-mentioned example of the square, its social efficacy certainly emanates from the actors and their means of distinction, while at the same time it would not be conceivable without the specific materiality of the square. The rededication of the square also makes it clear that change is always possible—in this case, resulting from the interplay of physical intervention and social interaction. Furthermore, in the process of arranging, synthesis and spacing are always tied to natural conditions as well: "Where there is no river, it cannot be included in the constitution of space" (Ibid., p. 161).

The problem with this understanding is that it includes a major inconsistency in comparison with Bourdieu's concept of space: The reciprocity described here does not include his juxtaposition of a metaphorically deployed social space and the appropriated physical space. While in social space, social processes are carried out and change is possible, in Bourdieu's understanding physical space merely absorbs these processes. As physical space is not considered as something that can influence social action, the structuring effect of spaces can only be thought of in terms of the aforementioned reinforcement effects (e.g., club effect), but not as something that has a fundamental influence on human action. Spaces that result from action cannot be compared to society as an outcome, but are to be understood as part of this process. Löw herself clearly expresses the discrepancy on this point: "Bourdieu's equation of structures with 'principles of class society' make it systematically impossible to study spatial structures as social phenomena. In this model of thinking, space and society are opposed to each other, whereby only society seems to shape space, not vice versa spaces pre-structure social processes" (Ibid., p. 141). There are many approaches in socialisation and education studies, particularly in the fields of environmental or architectural psychology (Hellbrück and Fischer 1999; Bär 2008) or also in the examination of a materially designed learning environment (Petmecky 2008), that have the physical-material environment as their starting point. If we modify Bourdieu's dictum, according to which the "habitat follows the habitus" (Bourdieu 1991, p. 32; cf. also Bourdieu and Wacquant 2013, p. 262), and also consider the reverse conclusion, it is possible to fit Bourdieu's logic of reproduction into the broad framework of Löw's sociology of space.

Löw herself makes repeated use of Bourdieu's concepts regarding habitus and the logic of reproduction, understanding it primarily as a factor in the constitution of space and less as a condition for social participation in space. Her chapter on "Space and Social Inequality" (Löw 2016, p. 177ff) breaks down the opportunities to constitute space according to wealth, knowledge, rank and association. On the side of action, it highlights the unequal opportunities to constitute space, while also suggesting that there are attributions and atmospheric qualities inherent in the outcome that produce effects of inclusion and exclusion, again coupled with different possibilities for space constitution (Ibid., p. 180f). This addresses essential conditions for capital acquisitions on a general level, as every constitution process ultimately results in built structures, produces instituionalised spaces and causes processes of exclusion and perception; it does not, however, offer a clear view of the (produced) structures and the opportunities and restrictions they entail. The focus of this section is not the creation of these social structures, but the opportunities of acquiring education and rising socially within them, from the perspective of the agent and under the aspect of accessibility.

For the discussion of the facilitating and limiting structures for capital acquisition (economic, social, cultural), three dimensions of a spatial influence are distinguished in the form of synthesis. These focus on both the physical and social accessibility of resources, summarising the aspects of regimentation addressed in Löw's and Bourdieu's relational and reproductive understandings, respectively. The focus is on the acting subject, whose possibilities of action and of acquiring capital depend on the respective habitus as well as the resources available. Physically bound to one's quarter or temporally to several places (action spaces), he is faced in spatial terms with a specific opportunity structure, which has been described with its neighbourhood and site effects and their numerous amplifications. Based on the ideal of social advancement and with a limited degree of mobility, he is confronted with fundamental obstacles in real space when it comes to obtaining capital:

First, access to resources that are relevant for advancement is physically regulated. From the point of view of the low-capital milieus, the acquisition of cultural and social capital presupposes contact points that convey codes relevant for upward mobility and rules of behaviour and facilitate networks across social milieus. The growing privatisation and regulation of urban space makes it more and more difficult to gain access to places and people and, to quote Lefebvre, raises the question of the "right to the city" (Holm and Gebhard 2011; Harvey 2008). Numerous levels of a limitation of action spaces can be identified—from bouncers at restaurants to fenced-in gated communities—largely relegating the capital-poor segments of the population to the (diminished) opportunity structure of their own neighbourhood. For an understanding of the selective accessibility of (urban) space it is significant that its constitution can take place over great distances. While Löw provides the conceptual framework with her relational perspective, she does not delve further into the agency of external actors, whose spacing and operation of synthesis through investments, location decisions, political influence or mobilisation of other actors in the global context and under market economy conditions have an enabling or limiting effect. According to Löw, the constitution of space is always pre-structured by social structures and the conditions of a situation of action, while these conditions depend to a "not inconsiderable extent on the actions of others" (Löw 2016, p. 163). Such a causal link can easily obscure the fact that the abolition of the principle of spatial proximity facilitates a complex logic of constitution whose cause-effect relationships can no longer be reconstructed. In a global context, the production of the socialisation context is lost (Scheffer and Voss 2008). Bourdieu does not account for the structuring effect of spaces, ignoring any external, global influence on options for action. His focus on capital-dependent positioning in social space and the emphasis on processes of separation, resulting in the occupation of physical localities, leaves no room for the creation of spatial conditions beyond individual positioning. In fact, there is an increasing polarisation when it comes to the accessibility of the resources of physical space, exhibiting different qualities that result not only from the lack of social appropriation on the part of groups that do not belong to a certain milieu, but from an economic concept. Large-scale "spacing" can mean that entry controls, forms of construction with a deterring effect, and locked gates result in a sorting of resources without identifiable actors and explanations. The same applies to the allocation of housing, and with it the opportunity for capital acquisition in a globalised real estate market. While gentrification, displacement and structural change take place within a certain neighbourhood, they can only be explained in the context of a bigger picture. Particularly in cities, the capitalisation of space has progressed to the point where it pre-structures individual opportunities to acquire capital from afar through power and property relations. For the disadvantaged segments of the population, this loss of the ability to understand why they are denied certain resources further curtails their influence on a constitution of space favourable to them.

The selective accessibility of localities with the resources relevant for upward mobility is also owed to the fact that they are too far away for disadvantaged segments of the population. In the urban context, proponents of the so-called mobility paradigm in particular have emphasised the importance of mobility for social constitution in general, stressing in particular the opportunity to overcome distance for obtaining resources (Urry 2007; Sheller 2014). Processes of residential segregation or poor infrastructure and transportation connections mean that someone's physical location in space carries a great deal of relevance. For people living in the periphery of a city, educational activities such as theatre or museum visits in the city centre involve a much greater effort than for residents of the city centre. The social composition of care and educational facilities is determined by the respective catchment area, and leisure activities are often based on what the residential environment offers. Unequal access to resources is particularly evident when viewing the locations of capital acquisition in a cross-regional perspective. Bourdieu's (1999) examples are strongly based on the view of the neighbourhood resident with a specific access to urban space. This obscures the fact that social stratification takes place in all spheres of life at different spatial levels involving considerable, socially exclusionary distances: From Aspen to St. Barth, the leisure and vacation industry alone has produced countless enclaves worldwide that, thanks to the homogeneity of their visitors, contribute to a capital increase within the group. The exchange of codes, trends and tastes, the creation of new networks and mutual self-assurance take place here under total exclusion. Their remoteness alone makes these places inaccessible to those who lack economic capital; neither structural barriers nor expensive infrastructure are necessary to prevent curious outsiders from entering the spheres where Bourdieu's club effects take effect. A spacing guaranteeing exclusivity for both the supply and demand side reproduces these club effects through spatial and social distancing.

Second, the use of resources is always socially pre-structured by the ability to perceive them. As has been repeatedly emphasised with reference to Bourdieu, access to the socio-spatial opportunity structure of a city is subject to the dispositions of habitus. The awareness itself that the opportunity for capital acquisition is unequally distributed spatially and that any conscious appropriation requires first and foremost the perception of profitable contact fields in the urban space, varies between individuals and classes. Recent publications on spatial and social mobility, therefore, analyse the influence of socialisation and education on the perception of spaces, placing their accessibility in the context of an individual's mobility in relation to their biography (Holz-Rau and Scheiner 2015). Hurrelmann's productive reality processing as a permanent confrontation with inner reality clearly emphasises the physical and social environment in the socialisation process (Hurrelmann and Bauer 2018). The active and independent appropriation of space (as part of the appropriation of external reality), which increases over time as the radius of action grows, has an effect on personality in that it affects a person's mobility (Döring 2015). In this process, socio-spatial experiences create individual templates of perception that can recursively encourage mobility and open up specific sites of capital acquisition, or—conversely—limit everyday actions to a framework that lacks resources relevant for upward mobility. Sufficient reference has been made to unequal socialisation conditions based on the family environment, residential location and amenities, numerous site effects and differences in mobility. It goes without saying that the way we perceive spatially distant things and contexts is fundamentally different from the way we perceive what is near to us. For the appropriation of (spatially distant) resources, however, this difference in perception resulting from a peripheral residential location or the ritualised frequenting of places far from capital, is crucial. As analyses from social psychology show, spatial distance is associated with a high degree of mental abstraction. It diminished the ability to grasp circumstances in a concrete and contextual way (e.g., Henderson et al. 2011). Without spatial approximation, a perceptual overgeneralisation of the "world of others" takes place, making the specific logic of recognition and exchange unintelligible to urban residents from other neighbourhoods. In contrast, those who are in the right space can perceive the system in a way that increases capital.

Löw, who devotes a separate section to perception, also emphasises the selectivity of perception as a function of habitus, education and socialisation (Löw 2016, p. 166). The perceptual activity of the person doing the constituting encompasses all senses that are activated when social goods and other people are exposed to the outside world (Ibid., p. 161). This means that beyond the visual perception of the material, there are also olfactory, haptic or acoustic impressions that influence the constitution of space. In relation to the restrictions in the process of capital acquisition, this once again addresses the habitually internalised perceptual filters and relevance criteria that make it easier or more difficult for individuals to register relevant spaces as such (operation of synthesis) or to influence spaces through actions in a way that promotes capital (spacing). As mentioned in the example of the rededicated square, it is not only physical objects but also smells or atmospheres that create distinction or create rejection and exclusion.

As a *third* point, social accessibility as a further restriction on capital acquisition shall be highlighted. As elaborated by Bourdieu, lack of access results from the lack of being able to use a spatially accessible offer of resources with the dispositions available. Here, habitus does not refer specifically to perception, but to the respective behavioural patterns, preferences and relevance criteria, which in many cases cannot connect to the socio-spatial conditions of a locality, or do so insufficiently. The expectations that everyone there is confronted with, whether in terms of language, dress or the concerns and interests presented, prevent meaningful contact if they are not met (e.g., Bourdieu 1991, p. 32). On the basis of his numerous examples, Bourdieu suggests that the capital-dependent segmentation of (urban) space with its implicit specifications regarding habitus is not limited to luxury or poor neighbourhoods, but in principle takes effect at all levels (especially Bourdieu 1999). For the capital-rich milieus, expensive stores, hotels, parks and exclusive leisure facilities could be mentioned in addition to educational institutions, museums, casinos and theatres. Even though they are open to the public, their use takes place in a very selective manner, as people lack the interest and cultural capital to be able to understand and appropriate the resources available there. Regardless of all further possibilities of differentiating such places, in the current moment the question could always be asked whether these specific expectation contexts must necessarily coincide with access to capital. For Bourdieu, the hierarchisation of space and the unequal distribution of capital has an official high culture as its norm, while specific offers beyond this norm may also promise capital acquisition (see also Schroer 2006, p. 105). Following this idea, well-paid fields of work in the creative sector could also be named for the present, which connect precisely to subcultural contexts and which can reward alternative or improvised lifestyles. Their codes and expectations toward outsiders might be less strict or show a greater tolerance for deviance. However, broader possibilities of connection for a disadvantaged urban population do not contradict Bourdieu's fundamental thesis, according to which permanent processes of demarcation reproducing the habitus occur in different social fields. This demarcation is not overcome by spatial proximity. Rather, a more intense contact in places outside one's own milieu makes it all the more apparent that stable social and spatial arrangements exist there that make it difficult for outsiders to gain a foothold (see also Berger et al. 2002; Ridgeway 2014). For the acquisition of social capital, Rutten et al. (2010) summarise accordingly: "In sum, the fact that human beings are spatially sticky and the fact that geographical proximity greatly enhances both the frequency and the depth of social interaction make that the norms and values aspect of social capital are spatially sticky as well. This aspect of social capital, therefore, is very difficult to tap into for outsiders, which makes it a powerful source of local competitive advantage" (Rutten et al. 2010, p. 869).

Several further effects can result from the above-mentioned three restrictions. A lack of physical access to certain places undoubtedly affects how they are perceived. Options that are inaccessible in an urban resident's daily life and are simply non-existent as an external reality, cannot increase social and cultural capital in the socialisation process. The result is the consolidation of a habitus that is less and less able to connect to the resources that are relevant for advancement. Spatial arrangements perpetuate these reproductive patterns, while the possibility of a spatial constitution more conducive to resource acquisition is compromised by habitus and its influence on spacing and operation of synthesis, as well as by the power of other, in some cases global actors.

2.4 Interim Conclusion: The Spatial Deprivation of Opportunities

The disintegration of society into a rich minority on the one hand and growing precariousness on the other, as has been registered for Germany and many other countries, harbours a high potential for conflict especially when it seems to become structurally entrenched. Starting with the proposition that education is the "…most important () basis for the material prosperity of modern societies" (Hradil 2001, p. 149), countless studies document an entrenched inequality of opportunity: Educational success correlates with social background, and social disadvantage pervades across generations. A discussion of inequality of opportunity in education must look at socialisation influences in general, including the reproductive patterns at work. Such an analysis must face a fundamental contradiction: While over the last decades, more and more people have had the chance to shape their own careers, only few have managed to move up in society. While according to Hurrelmann and Bauer (2018), the socialisation process as personality development takes place within the tension-laden framework of external and internal reality; Bourdieu (1983, 1984, 1991) in particular offers a well-established pattern of analysis, with his distinction between the types of capital and the dispositions of the habitus, both as components and products of socialisation: Widely used empirically, it shows how groups and individuals in the social field seek to distinguish themselves from one another through practices and how the validity of the prevailing rules and expectations shape habitus. The latter is expressed in physical and cognitive dispositional patterns that find acceptance only in specific contexts. They work well within a milieu, but set boundaries in relation to others, thus illuminating the logic of social reproduction.

On this basis, it has been argued that it is particularly the spatial context that perpetuates inequality of opportunity. If, in addition, we understand the constitution of spaces as an expression of social processes and focus on their creation through actions, then this resource-dependent constitution performance results in a further dimension of social permanence: The many advantages and disadvantages that exist in (urban) space as a result of the social and physical environment (accessibility, recreational value, contact opportunities, etc.) must then be understood not only as the result of actions, but at the same time as essential conditions for the constitution of space. Looked at from this vantage point, the options for action of the privileged population are further strengthened: Having resources at one's disposition favours a spatial design that in turn facilitates resource acquisition. By analogy, this applies to disadvantaged population groups with the opposite effect.

The relational understanding of space elaborated in Löw's Sociology of Space (2016) as the arrangement of living beings and social goods in places constituted by synthesis and spacing accordingly presents space as a dimension of structure and action. Bourdieu's concept of habitus can be linked to Löw by amplifying his understanding that social processes shape space in the sense that the inverse is also true and spaces pre-structure social processes. Habitus influences perception and possibilities of spacing, while at the same time habitus is formed in the context of physical-material conditions, specific sensory impressions and the social contexts of the spatial environment at different stages of life. The reproduction of social inequality becomes comprehensible if we trace the separation of resources relevant for upward mobility—and this includes all of Bourdieu's forms of capital—in a spatial perspective. Among disadvantaged milieus, there is a lack of experience, contacts and educational opportunities in many areas of life. In contrast, resources are concentrated around privileged milieus. Spatial separation into contexts of perception and social action that have either a limiting or a promoting effect forces those without access to relate to their own milieus, thus reproducing social differences.

Larger cities in particular exhibit numerous contexts of a specifically perceived, differently effective and unequally accessible opportunity structure at various levels. It is revealed in the apartment building with a doorman, in the image of a neighbourhood, in the available transportation infrastructure, in the distribution of urban educational institutions, in the dress code of a casino or in the numerous addresses, often unknown to the general public, that provide a place of exchange for specific groups. Only by focusing on the ubiquity of concrete and abstract boundaries, of visible and invisible hurdles, can the socially reproducing structure of space be adequately captured.

To summarise, the lack of access to the sites of potential capital acquisition has been described in three dimensions: (a) physical accessibility, where borders, obstructions and spatial distances play a role; (b) the perception of spaces and resources; and (c) social distance in the sense of a lack of compatibility with implicit expectations. All three types of restrictions impact one another and different forms of capital are required to overcome them.

To complicate matters, these regulations are not only owed to the interests and power of actors that can be named and localised, but also to global utilisation contexts. This can affect physical accessibility (a) if, for example, gentrification processes, privatisation measures and the regulation of spaces or job relocations follow chained decisions and obey a global market logic. As a result of the transformation of socialisation contexts, perception and social accessibility (b and c) would be equally affected. We can therefore speak of a cross-border deprivation of spatial opportunities. This type of deprivation, in which the new information and communication technologies play a central role, is something that a single person cannot reconstruct. It creates a certain powerlessness on the already difficult path to acquiring resources relevant for advancement.

However, the idea that in the age of global interdependence, capital acquisition is also dependent on cross-border processes, could also be looked at from a different angle: Couldn't the new technologies, first and foremost the internet, also create a completely new path to the different types of capital? If we accept the relevance of the restrictions highlighted here in the spatial context, then it is necessary to examine the extent to which they can be overcome with the help of new internet-based options for action.

References

Ainsworth, James W. (2002): Why Does It Take a Village? The Mediation of Neighborhood Effects on Educational Achievement. *Social Forces* 81, 117–152.
Altrock, Uwe & Kunze, Ronald (Hrsg.) (2017): *Stadterneuerung und Armut. Jahrbuch Stadterneuerung 2016*. Wiesbaden: Springer VS.
Atkinson, Anthony B.; Piketty, Thomas & Saez, Emmanuel (2011): Top Incomes in the Long Run of History. *Journal of Economic Literature* 49 (1), 3–71.
Autor, David; Katz, Lawrence & Krueger, Alan B. (1999): Computing Inequality: Have Computers Changed the Labor Market? *Quarterly Journal of Economics* 113, 1169–1214.
Bär, Paul Klaus-Dieter (2008): *Architekturpsychologie. Psychosoziale Aspekte des Wohnens*. Gießen: Psychosozial-Verlag.
Bennett, Tony; Savage, Mike; Silva, Elizabeth; Warde, Alan; Gayo-Cal, Modesto & Wright, David (2009): *Culture, Class, Distinction*. New York: Routledge.
Benson, Michaela; Bridge, Gary & Wilson, Deborah (2015): School Choice in London and Paris—A Comparison of Middle-Class Strategies. *Social Policy & Administration* 49 (1), 24–43.
Berger, Joseph; Ridgeway, Cecilia, L. & Zelditch, Morris (2002): Construction of Status and Referential Structures. *Sociological Theory* 20 (2), 157–179.
Biermann, Ralf (2009): Die Bedeutung des Habitus-Konzepts für die Erforschung soziokultureller Unterschiede im Bereich der Medienpädagogik. *MedienPädagogik* 17, 1–18.
Blasius, Jörg; Friedrichs, Jürgen & Klöckner, Jennifer (2008): *Doppelt benachteiligt? Leben in einem deutsch-türkischen Stadtteil*. Wiesbaden: Springer VS.
Bound, John & Johnson, George (1992): Changes in the Structure of Wages in the 1980s: An Evaluation of Alternative Explanations. *American Economic Review* 83, 371–392.
Bourdieu, Pierre (1979): *Entwurf einer Theorie der Praxis auf der ethnologischen Grundlage der Kabylischen Gesellschaft*. Frankfurt a. M.: Suhrkamp.
Bourdieu, Pierre (1983): Ökonomisches Kapital, kulturelles Kapital, soziales Kapital. In: Reinhard Kreckel (Hrsg.): Soziale Ungleichheiten. Göttingen: Schwartz, S. 183–198.
Bourdieu, Pierre (1984): *Distinction. A Social Critique of the Judgement of Taste*. New York, London: Routledge.
Bourdieu, Pierre (1991): Physischer, sozialer und angeeigneter physischer Raum. In: Martin Wentz (Hrsg.): *Stadt-Räume*. Frankfurt a. M.: Campus Verlag, 25–34.
Bourdieu, Pierre (1999): *The Weight of the World: Social Suffering in Contemporary Society*. Stanford, CA.: Stanford University Press.

Bourdieu, Pierre & Wacquant, Loïc (2013): *Reflexive Anthropologie*. Frankfurt a. M.: Suhrkamp.
Castel, Robert (2000): *Die Metamorphosen der sozialen Frage*. Konstanz: UVK Verlagsgesellschaft.
Castells, Manuel (2009): *The Rise of the Network Society*. Vol. 1. Hoboken: Wiley-Blackwell.
Chancel, Lucas; Piketty, Thomas; Saez, Emmanuel & Zucman, Gabriel (2022): *World Inequality Report 2022*. Cambridge: Harvard University Press.
Cucca, Roberta & Ranci, Costanzo (2017): *Unequal Cities: The Challenge of Post-industrial Transition in Times of Austerity*. London: Routledge.
Cushion, Christopher J. & Jones, Robyn L. (2012): A Bourdieusian Analysis of Cultural Reproduction: Socialisation and the 'Hidden Curriculum' in Professional Football. *Sport, Education and Society* 19 (3), 276–298.
Dangschat, Jens S. (2017): Armut und Stadterneuerung - zwei Seiten einer Medallie? In: Uwe Altrock & Ronald Kunze (eds.): *Stadterneuerung und Armut. Jahrbuch Stadterneuerung 2016*. Wiesbaden: Springer VS, 13–35.
De Maio, Fernando G. & Benjamins, Maureen R. (eds.) (2021): *Unequal Cities: Structural Racism and the Death Gap in America's 30 Largest Cities*. Baltimore: Johns Hopkins University Press.
Deffner, Veronika & Haferburg, Christoph. (2012): Raum, Stadt und Machtverhältnisse. Humangeographische Auseinandersetzungen mit Bourdieu. *Geographische Zeitschrift* 100 (3), 164–180.
Deutsche Bundesbank (2022): Eine verteilungsbasierte Vermögensbilanz der privaten Haushalte in Deutschland – Ergebnisse und Anwendungen. Monatsbericht Juni 2022. online: https://www.bundesbank.de/resource/blob/894880/958edb67dec48f1dbdeccaf0efd36768/mL/2022-07-vermoegensbilanz-data.pdf (1 March 2023).
Dimaggio, Paul. (1979). On Pierre Bourdieu. Review Essay on Outline of a Theory of Practice by Pierre Bourdieu and Reproduction: In Education, Society and Culture by Pierre Bourdieu and Jean-Claude Passeron. *American Journal of Sociology* 84 (6), 80–86.
Döring, Lisa (2015): Biografieeffekte und intergenerationale Sozialisationseffekte in Mobilitätsbiografien. In: Joachim Scheiner & Christian Holz-Rau (eds.): *Räumliche Mobilität und Lebenslauf*. Wiesbaden: Springer VS, 23–41.
Druyen, Thomas C. J.; Lauterbach, Wolfgang & Grundmann, Matthias (eds.) (2009): *Reichtum und Vermögen. Zur gesellschaftlichen Bedeutung von Reichtums- und Vermögensforschung*. Wiesbaden: Springer VS.
Ecarius, Jutta; Köbel, Nils & Wahl, Katrin (2011): *Familie, Erziehung und Sozialisation*. Wiesbaden: Springer VS.
Florida, Richard; Adler, Patrick & Mellander, Charlotta (2017): The City as Innovation Machine. *Regional Studies* 51 (1), 86–96.

Frick, Joachim R. & Grabka, Markus M. (2009): Zur Entwicklung der Vermögensungleichheit in Deutschland. *Berlin Journal für Soziologie* 19 (4), 577–600.

Giddens, Anthony (1984): *The Constitution of Society. Outline of the Theory of Structuration.* Cambridge: Polity Press.

Gornig, Martin & Goebel, Jan (2013): Ökonomischer Strukturwandel und Polarisierungstendenzen in deutschen Stadtregionen. In: Martin Kronauer & Walter Siebel (Hrsg.): *Polarisierte Städte. Soziale Ungleichheit als Herausforderung für die Stadtpolitik.* Frankfurt a. M.: Campus Verlag, S. 51–68.

Graham, Mark & Anwar, Mohammad Amir (2019): Labour. In: James Ash, Rob Kitchin & Agnieszka Leszczynski (eds.): *Digital Geographies.* Los Angeles: Sage, 177–187.

Haandrikman, Karen; Costa, Rafael; Malmberg, Bo; Rogne, Adrian Farner & Sleutjes, Bart (2023): Socio-economic Segregation in European Cities. A Comparative Study of Brussels, Copenhagen, Amsterdam, Oslo and Stockholm. *Urban Geography* 44 (1), 1–36.

Harvey, David (2008): The Right to the City. *New Left Review* 53, 23–40.

Häußermann, Hartmut & Siebel, Walter (2004): *Stadtsoziologie. Eine Einführung.* Frankfurt a. M.: Campus Verlag.

Hellbrück, Jürgen & Fischer, Manfred (1999): *Umweltpsychologie. Ein Lehrbuch.* Göttingen: Hogrefe Verlag.

Henderson, Marlone D.; Wakslak, Cheryl J.; Fujita, Kentaro & Rohrbach, John (2011): Construal Level Theory and Spatial Distance. *Social Psychology* 42 (3), 165–173.

Holm, Andrej & Gebhardt, Dirk (2011): *Initiativen für ein Recht auf Stadt. Theorie und Praxis städtischer Aneignung.* Hamburg: VSA-Verlag.

Holt, Douglas B. (1997): Distinction in America? Recovering Bourdieu's Theory of Tastes from Its Critics. *Poetics* 25, 93–120.

Holz-Rau, Christian & Scheiner, Joachim (2015): Mobilitätsbiografien und Mobilitätssozialisation: Neue Zugänge zu einem alten Thema. In: Joachim Scheiner & Christian Holz-Rau (eds.): *Räumliche Mobilität und Lebenslauf.* Wiesbaden: Springer VS, 3–22.

Hradil, Stefan (2001): *Soziale Ungleichheit in Deutschland.* Wiesbaden: Springer VS.

Hurrelmann, Klaus & Bauer, Ullrich (2018): *Socialisation During the Life Course.* New York, London: Routledge.

Kakwani, Nanak (2022): *Economic Inequality and Poverty Facts, Methods, and Policies.* Oxford: Oxford University Press.

King, Anthony (2000): Thinking with Bourdieu Against Bourdieu: A „Practical" Critique of the Habitus. *Sociological Theory* 18 (3), 417–433.

Kreckel, Reinhard (1992): *Politische Soziologie der sozialen Ungleichheit.* Frankfurt a. M.: Campus Verlag.

Kronauer, Martin & Siebel, Walter (eds.) (2013): *Polarisierte Städte. Soziale Ungleichheit als Herausforderung für die Stadtpolitik*. Frankfurt a. M.: Campus Verlag.

Kronauer, Martin & Vogel, Martin (2004): Erfahrung und Bewältigung von sozialer Ausgrenzung in der Großstadt: Was sind Quartierseffekte, was Lageeffekte? In: Hartmut Häußermann, Martin Kronauer & Walter Siebel (eds.): *An den Rändern der Städte. Armut und Ausgrenzung*. Frankfurt a. M.: Suhrkamp, 235–257.

Lampert, Thomas & Rosenbrock, Rolf (2017): Armut und Gesundheit. In: Der Paritätische Gesamtverband (eds.): *Bericht zur Armutsentwicklung in Deutschland 2017*. Berlin, 98–108.

Lauen, Lee (2016): Contextual Explanations of School Choice. *Sociology of Education* 80 (3), 179–209.

Levy, Frank & Murnane, Richard J. (1992): U.S. Earnings and Earnings Inequality: A Review of Recent Trends and Proposed Explanations. *Journal of Economic Literature* 30, 1333–1381.

Löw, Martina (2016): *The Sociology of Space: Materiality, Social Structures, and Action*. New York: Palgrave Macmillan.

Mackert, Jürgen (ed.) (2004): *Die Theorie sozialer Schließung. Tradition, Analysen, Perspektiven*. Wiesbaden: Springer VS.

Miethe, Ingrid; Tervooren, Anja & Ricken, Norbert (eds.) (2017): *Bildung und Teilhabe*. Wiesbaden: Springer VS.

Musterd, Sako; Marcińczak, Szymon; van Ham, Maarten & Tammaru, Tiit (2017): Socioeconomic Segregation in European Capital Cities: Increasing Separation Between Poor and Rich. *Urban Geography* 38 (7), 1062–1083.

OECD (2018): *Divided Cities. Understanding Intra-urban Inequalities*. Paris: OECD Publishing.

Petmecky, Andrea (2008): *Architektur von Entwicklungsumwelten. Umweltaneignung und -wahrnehmung im Kindergarten*. Marburg: Tectum-Verlag.

Piketty, Thomas (2014): *Capital in the Twenty-First Century*. Cambridge: Harvard University Press.

Piketty, Thomas & Saez, Emmanuel (2006): The Evolution of Top Incomes: A Historical and International Perspective. *American Economic Review* 96 (2), 200–205.

Prieur, Annick; Rosenlund, Lennart & Skjott-Larsen, Jakob (2008): Cultural Capital Today: A Case Study from Denmark. *Poetics* 36, 45–71.

Quillian, Lincoln & Lagrange, Hugues (2016): Socioeconomic Segregation in Large Cities in France and the United States. *Demography* 53 (4), 1051–1084.

Ridgeway, Claudia (2014): Why Status Matters for Inequality. *American Sociological Review* 79 (1), 1–16.

Rohrbach, Daniela (2008): *Wissensgesellschaft und soziale Ungleichheit. Ein Zeit- und Ländervergleich*. Wiesbaden: Springer VS.

Rössel, Jörg (2009): *Sozialstrukturanalyse. Eine kompakte Einführung*. Wiesbaden: Springer VS.
Rutten, Roel; Westlund, Hans & Boekema, Frans (2010): The Spatial Dimension of Social Capital. *European Planning Studies* 18 (6), 863–871.
Sassen, Saskia (1994): *Cities in a World Economy: Sociology for a New Century*. Thousand Oaks, London, New Dehli: Sage.
Sassen, Saskia (2001): *The Global City*. New York, London, Tokyo. Princeton: Princeton University Press.
Scheffer, Jörg & Voss, Martin (2008): Die Privatisierung der Sozialisation - Der Soziale Raum als heimlicher Lehrplan im Wandel. In: Petia Genkova (ed.): *Erfolg durch Schlüsselqualifikationen? "heimliche Lehrpläne" und Basiskompetenzen im Zeichen der Globalisierung*. Lengerich: Pabst Science Publishers, 102–115.
Schroer, Markus (2006): *Räume, Orte, Grenzen. Auf dem Weg zu einer Soziologie des Raums*. Frankfurt a. M.: Suhrkamp.
Schürz, Martin (2016): Die Rückkehr der sozialen Frage. *Zeitschrift für Individualpsychologie* 41 (3), 197–206.
Sheller, Mimi (2014): The New Mobilities Paradigm for a Live Sociology. *Current Sociology Review* 62 (6), 789–811.
Siebel, Walter (2012): Stadt und soziale Ungleichheit. *Leviathan* 40 (3), 462–475.
United Nations (2020): World Social Report 2020. Inequality in a rapidly changing world. online: https://www.un.org/development/desa/dspd/wp-content/uploads/sites/22/2020/02/World-Social-Report2020-FullReport.pdf. (1 March 2023)
Urry, John (2007): *Mobilities*. Cambridge: Polity.

Open Access This chapter is licensed under the terms of the Creative Commons Attribution 4.0 International License (http://creativecommons.org/licenses/by/4.0/), which permits use, sharing, adaptation, distribution and reproduction in any medium or format, as long as you give appropriate credit to the original author(s) and the source, provide a link to the Creative Commons license and indicate if changes were made.

The images or other third party material in this chapter are included in the chapter's Creative Commons license, unless indicated otherwise in a credit line to the material. If material is not included in the chapter's Creative Commons license and your intended use is not permitted by statutory regulation or exceeds the permitted use, you will need to obtain permission directly from the copyright holder.

CHAPTER 3

Digital and Digitised Space as an Opportunity for Advancement

Abstract This chapter analyses the terms of action and structures in the virtual space, comparing them with the rules of the real space. The initial separation between real space and cyberspace is artificial yet intentional, with the aim of illustrating space-related opportunities. A view of the new opportunities in connection with digitalised reals spaces, and in particular with virtual spaces, also includes the problem that obtaining digital contents can be realised in society only in an unequal manner. In this context, educational research has identified serious limitations which are identified as digital divides and will be looked at from different angles. Incorporating these findings, it will be examined to what extent digitalisation can withstand the previously highlighted restrictions of capital accumulation and in which areas of daily life it is possible to dissolve the existing spatial and social rules.

Keywords Digital space · Digital divide · Digital unequalities · Digital learning

The growing networking of computers and the establishment of browsers and the World Wide Web in the early 1990s were perceived early on in the social sciences as drivers of social change processes: It was believed that if the limitations of natural communication were replaced by a mode of exchange where spatial distance no longer plays a role, this would result in an enormous increase of options for each user. New ways of relating to the world would open up and things like work, the neighbourhood in which one lived, friendships or available educational institutions—things that had been determined by spatial proximity since time immemorial—would need to be reassessed in light of global networking (Rheingold 1994; Negroponte 1995). The technological accessibility of the world was equated with new options for action, hailed by the globalisation discourse of the late 1990s.

In the past two decades, academic research on these new conditions has gained more and more momentum, while at the same time the Internet as the object of research has changed rapidly. Whereas the nodes of the digital network used to be computers that users had to operate in a fixed location, they have now become powerful small devices such as smartphones, tablets or wearables that users carry with them. Whereas access to the world used to take place through the use of a keyboard or display, now voice commands, gestures or, increasingly, the mere passing of sensors are enough to trigger automated processes. Whereas until the turn of the millennium the content of the Internet was more like a showcase that could be furnished only by experts, it has since become a participatory and collaborative space (Web 2.0), facilitating the breakthrough of numerous platforms and social networks. Thanks to the recent development toward a semantic web (often headlined as Web 3.0), which contextualises queries and automatically recognises relevance contexts, the growing use of artificial intelligence and, last but not least, the increasing penetration of networked objects into everyday life (Internet of Things), users seem to be empowered even further. As new digital spaces are opening up, mediatisation is becoming a social metaprocess that determines how people communicate (Hahn 2021).

The transformation toward a "digital society" (Housley et al. 2022) will continue and business representatives, scholars and politicians all stress the importance of IT skills as key competencies. However, the question remains if digitalisation can help to break the patterns of the stratification processes shown here.

In a spatial perspective, the question of the importance of digital skills for capital acquisition can first be considered in an extended real space: A change in the quality of everyday life as a result of IT services and the growing connectivity of things should have an impact on the individual's options for perception and action. From low-cost ride sharing services to remote control of household functions or the use of data glasses—all these innovations can help users save money and provide them with contact opportunities or new stimuli, facilitating the acquisition of capital in real space. However, it is by no means clear whether this changes anything about the important connection between everyday spaces of action and the possibility of obtaining resources relevant for advancement. Ultimately, users of modern technologies, as they are physically present in real space, continue to be subject to the same socialisation conditions that have shaped their habitus.

This changes in a situation where people have the option to temporarily withdraw from the real world, while they are still able to obtain essential resources: In cyberspace or virtual space, numerous everyday activities such as shopping, playing games, bookings, maintaining contacts or attending classes can be carried out digitally. Its terms are fundamentally different from real space. Place and time become less significant; what is more, as no other person is physically present, the form of communication, its intensity and commitment all obtain a different quality. It could be argued that local effects tend to lose their influence in this virtual sphere. With its low threshold, cyberspace offers the opportunity to become familiar with the rules, tastes and conventions of distant milieus and then make use of the acquired competencies in real space. Part of such a strategy can be a vigorous self-education, which also seems to be obtainable via numerous offers on the Internet, independent of space, anonymously and at low cost.

Furthermore, the conditions for the constitution of space in the virtual sphere could also be very different from the regulations of real space. A greater influence of disadvantaged population groups could help create a parallel world with fewer hierarchies, providing individuals with convertible resources regardless of their milieu.

This section will therefore examine action and structure in virtual space in more detail, comparing it with the regulations of the physical real space described above. To begin with, an artificial distinction between physical space and cyberspace will be made to help illustrate space-related opportunities. Subsequently, the numerous links between physical real space and cyberspace will be analysed, focusing on the growing use of intelligent control mechanisms in real space as well as the possibility of influencing real space from cyberspace.

Finally, when we consider the new potentials related to digitalised real space and, in particular, virtual space, it must be taken into account that obtaining digital content is possible across society only in an unequal manner. Research in the field of education has identified considerable limitations, which are referred to and analysed as digital divides or digital inequalities. Taking these findings into account, the goal will be to explore the extent to which digitalisation can nevertheless defy the restrictions on capital acquisition that have been highlighted, and in which areas of everyday life the spatial-social regimentation can possibly be dissolved.

3.1 Transformations into the Virtual: Structure and Plot

Spatial structures condition processes of education and upward mobility in a special way. As has been shown, with respect to real space this is true for two reasons: For one, there are numerous site effects, and secondly, opportunities for a constitution of space conducive to advancement are inscribed in these structures. Since in a relational understanding of space which has been explored based on Löw´s theory, spatial structures are not given, but are constituted through action, reproduced in repetitive practices and anchored in institutions, they are to be understood as a reflection of unequal resources. The real space thus produced distorts the conditions for capital acquisition in both directions: It favours the privileged and hampers those segments of the population who lack capital. The spatial experience becomes entrenched and influences the habitus, which in turn determines patterns of perception and action. "The class-specific character of the spaces penetrates into the bodies" (Löw 2016, p. 149).

When we look at virtual space or cyberspace, the described conditions of structure and action described above take on a different meaning. Cyberspace provides an environment that can be used for economic-pragmatic, experimental or utopian purposes in equal measure. It shares some of the features of the Internet, which, as a global hypermedium of linked sites with texts, graphics, sounds and videos, also relies on the infrastructure of computer media, allowing for actions in the virtual sphere. Significant areas of cyberspace can be realised within the topography of networks of the World Wide Web. At the same time, cyberspace provides an even larger field of action in that it conveys the illusion of spatial depth and realistic motion sequences within as well as outside of the Internet. In addition to computer games and simulations, it involves virtual realities that allow for total immersion via glasses, data gloves or a 3D mouse. However, as will be discussed further, cyberspace mostly depends on the Internet to actually make relevant resources available.

As a constantly changing space that can be experienced on several levels simultaneously, it is useful to conceive of cyberspace relationally, in analogy to Löw's concept of space. Löw (2016) uses cyberspace as an example to counteract the absolutist/monolithic concept of space, tying it to the relational perspective: "When spaces are reified as territories or concrete places, the constitution of spaces in cyberspace is systematically excluded" (Löw 2016, p. 79). It is obvious that their constitution is also the result of the actions of individuals. However, the transfer of this terminology to cyberspace reveals blind spots that make it clear that Löw was less concerned with its conceptual integration (see also Herrmann 2010, p. 14). To begin with, Löw's main point of departure, defining space as a "relational arrangement of living beings and social goods in places" needs to be specified for the virtual sphere: Virtual arrangements do not refer to the physicality of living beings or physical conditions, but at best to their digital image. Thiedeke uses the term cybernetic sociofacts that result from encounters that take place in a virtualised environment, producing and reproducing a very different reality than physically bound individuals and artefacts (Thiedeke 2004, p. 16). He talks of "cybernetic sociofacts" encountering each other in a virtual environment, (re-)producing a reality that is very different from that of physically bound individuals and artefacts. It is a characteristic of cyberspace that it can be generated within its technical infrastructure solely by means of numbers, not requiring any digital representation of actual physical conditions. But since users have been socialised in real space, numerous translations of real space can be found in cyberspace to make it more relatable. Images are certainly helpful for finding one's way in the virtual parallel world, providing orientation and making cyberspace attractive as a copy. This virtual continuum is also structured by numerous spatial metaphors ("surfing", "firewall", "cloud", etc.), facilitating operation of synthesis there. In this sense, even localities which according to Löw are "the goal and result of placing", remain at best abstract analogies in the virtual sphere.

Since action that constitutes space is bound to the synthesis of what exists, virtual actions must also take place in a different mode. This also applies to building, erecting or spacing—processes that only allow for a conceptual transferability in cyberspace where virtual analogies to real space exist already. Moreover, action does not take place through appearing physically, as there are completely different potentials available in cyberspace. Processes of arranging are realised via clicks and mouse movements, sensors or touch screens at a high speed, there is the option of exact copiability, and access options are different. The constitution of space can even take place without any human action, as in virtual space new forms of interaction exist between technical artefacts, each with its own constitution performance (agents, avatars, or bots).

Apart from the need for specification in the transfer of Löw's sociology of space to cyberspace, the crucial question with reference to social stratification processes is about the fundamental opportunities for the constitution of space in cyberspace. At first glance, it is the users who constitute new digital spaces through their actions—producing websites, initiating forums and shaping the spatial structure of cyberspace with their own content.

On closer inspection, however, the possibility of constituting cyberspace is linked to further technical prerequisites. The individual and collaborative creation of spaces does not change the fact that this is possible only within an existing infrastructure, specific software and numerous technical components such as Internet protocols, algorithms, operating systems, platforms, networks and page configurations. Unlike real space, which is socially constructed and enables actions a priori, albeit in highly different ways, there is no virtual space outside of its technical infrastructure. Although it appears limitless and continues to expand rapidly, it relies on a man-made input which follows certain conditions. There are legal and technical limits to the creation of space and many activities are subject to an existing "code". "Out there on the electronic frontier, code is the law" (Mitchell 1996, p. 111). Beyond virtual space, the rules of the code reach into everyday life in real space and enable or impede actions that constitute space. Kitchin and Dodge (2011) have used numerous examples to examine the power of codes, illustrating how they have become embedded as hidden rules in numerous contexts. They distinguish between "coded space" and "code/space". Whereas coded space refers to a space in which the software assumes merely a supporting function (e.g., presentation software), code/space creates this space and its function. To give an example, without functioning technology a check-in counter at an airport would be nothing more than an unorganised collection of people. Here, spatiality is the product of the code (Ibid., p. 16). Despite its importance, code/space does not fundamentally determine the design of space, as a variety of spatial arrangements are conceivable depending on the context as well as the interactions of people, which can be irrational and unpredictable (Ibid., p. 18). Nevertheless, it is evident that the resource-based power to constitute space—online as well as offline—is effectively concentrated in the background, emanating in particular from those actors who have the means to access and shape the code. If we explore the question of causation further and ask about the respective origin of the code, the related distribution of power for the constitution process of space seems even less tangible than in the non-digital context that was described above. The exact composition and mode of action of the code itself is equally intransparent. In most cases, the user does not know what is stored by a data medium and who benefits from it and in what way. Authorship is blurred by different forms of participation—cloud providers, network operators, designers, developers or hackers, as well as the possibility of bringing about autonomous decision-making processes via artificial intelligence. In summary, an unequal distribution of power is undoubtedly inherent in cyberspace as well. However, the difficulty of locating this power additionally curtails users´ ability to orient themselves within the system, to make informed decisions and to deal with problems in ways that benefit them. For users who have the necessary skills, it is still possible to benefit from hegemonic code/space contexts (Zook and Graham 2018).

Ultimately, the possibility to participate in the constitution of cyberspace varies between different segments of the population, as it requires specific skills (such as the ability to program) or resources to influence the virtual environment. Such an influence can happen through purchasing technical infrastructure, acquiring web space or participating in a digital business model, which makes it clear that the actual constitution of space does not take place in cyberspace itself, but is controlled by hired programmers from real space. From there, it provides different frameworks of possibilities for users in cyberspace—from pre-programmed virtual reality games to the creation of a new website. Accordingly, the necessary resources one needs to shape the constitution process in the virtual sphere to one´s advantage are not fundamentally different from real space. Depending on one´s position in the system of the web economy, Bourdieu's types of capital are again helpful, whereas their individual significance may differ. While the head of an Internet company can influence cyberspace thanks to their contacts, financial means and education, the significance of these resources can diminish the closer one is to the actual programming work. For a professional programmer, someone who dabbles in IT as a hobby or is active as an independent hacker, specific programming skills diminish the importance of cultural and social capital. The stereotypical programmer nerd, isolated in a cold garage and living on delivered pizza and defying the usual conventions in appearance, language or personal hygiene, demonstrates that the acquisition of economic capital does not necessarily require social adjustment. The ability to constitute space becomes independent of the place of action. The "symbolic and material factors" emphasised by Löw, which can be found in a given situation of action (2016, p. 130f), lose their importance, as does the habitus of the agent that Löw also stresses. Nevertheless, as these and other examples from the new web economy demonstrate, there is no fundamental shift in opportunities in favour of the disadvantaged segments of the population. While the constitution of cyberspace follows different rules than those described by Löw for real space, it still presupposes very specific resources that, apart from IT experts, continue to be largely concentrated in the hands of capital-rich actors who can directly or indirectly influence the code.

In contrast, if we consider the *options for action* in cyberspace, there actually exist more opportunities for advancement. The scientific euphoria about its possibilities and the numerous opportunities for acquiring capital is based on characteristics that fundamentally distinguish cyberspace from physical space: For one thing, interaction and communication in virtual space are no longer tied to a specific temporal-spatial context. Users can establish a relationship across large spatial distances and without temporal offset. This implies a detachment of users from the social environment of real space and their emancipation from the influence of socially assigned places. In her sociology of space, Löw had emphasised this physical attachment as an essential regulative: "The body thus gains an essential significance in several respects. In the first place, people are physically in the world. They move and take place with the body. In the second place, the physical expression guides both the placements and the syntheses of other people. This bodily expression and its perception are permeated by the structural principles class and gender. The body is thus at the centre of many constitutions of space" (Löw 2016, p. 151). While not all actions in virtual space are independent of physical presence, especially those performed with the help of the Internet completely transcend physical and face-to-face forms of exchange.

In addition, cyberspace also breaks open the information and educational structure of real space by making available things that could not be accessed in the same way in the pre-digital age via books, newspapers or other media. However, it must be taken into account that the actual use of these offers often requires media transfers that lead back into real space. For example, a virtual job ad will usually lead to a face-to-face interview, and deeper social relationships rely on a physical presence preceding or following the virtual contact. After finding a new employee through the Internet, the employer will also expect a physical encounter, and the quality of the digitally acquired skills must be demonstrated in the real world. This does not change the fact that the opportunity of finding information and contacts digitally represents a historically unique potential, which can enable computer users to shed, at least partially, the isolating and limiting conditions of their place of origin.

Furthermore—and this appears to be a fundamental difference from physical space—cyberspace can be accessed and explored largely without any hierarchy, regardless of capital resources. Characteristics of inequality such as income, appearance or status are no longer relevant entry criteria in the virtual world. When it comes to the Internet, every user can navigate it without barriers and under the same conditions, is allowed to enter social meeting places or networks in the same way and can consume instructive content with the same comfort as every other user. As will be explained in more detail, the virtual movement between millions of pages in the virtual medium of the Internet does not take place in a completely unstructured space. Again, the mode defined in the (program) code has a fundamental effect on the user's actions by predetermining what can be done on which page. Furthermore, the link structure creates virtual neighbourhoods that can make it easier or harder to reach certain pages, tying the likelihood of access to visibility and perception. We will come back to this soft control later.

Overall, however, cyberspace is largely open in its layout. The divisions of real space discussed above, which create inequality between groups of people, as well as the unequal possibility of disposing of spaces as a resource (cf. Löw **2016**, p. 233), thus seem to play a lesser role in cyberspace.

For the time being, the following conclusion can be drawn. Although the conditions for the constitution of virtual space remain difficult, the threshold for action in virtual space is lower than for real space. Consequently, we can no longer assume a "duality of space" for cyberspace. This is where the transfer of Löw's concept is no longer useful, as the space-constituting actors act largely from real space, while cyberspace users can only take advantage of digital space once they "enter" it. As demonstrated, different conditions exist between spaces, which, depending on the focus of action, can override the reciprocal referentiality of action and structure.

In the further course of this chapter, we will put aside the rules of the space-constituting actors in order to explore the opportunities for capital acquisition in virtual space. In concrete terms, the three dimensions of restrictions in social space and disadvantages in real space which have been diagnosed can be applied to cyberspace.

3.2 Capital Acquisition in Cyberspace

In contrast to the numerous disadvantages that limit the inhabitant of an urban residential area in the form of physical (health limitations, lack of infrastructure, structural deficiencies, etc.), social or psychological characteristics (social environment, a feeling of confinement, image, etc.), the aim so far has been to capture more fundamentally why social advancement is difficult for the resource-poor sections of the population. Space in its reproducing function, as a condition and result of action, has been the main focus, arguing that the constitution of space results from actions which deprive disadvantaged segments of the population of resources relevant for advancement. Spaces and, more concretely, places as unique and specifically designated sections of space, are mainly based on the interests of capital-strong actors. They are constituted as part of an economic logic of utilisation, and it is no longer possible to understand relations of cause and effect solely in a local context. Amidst such complexity, it is difficult to capture and to act against the disadvantages that result from them. The inability to improve one´s situation is perceived as fateful as abstract market forces negatively impact an individual´s spatial opportunity structure. The resignation in the face of existing spatial conditions corresponds with the general acceptance of the existing order as described by Bourdieu (Doxa) (cf. 1979, S. 322–330). As is true for the spatial environment, this order is perceived as normal and therefore—just like the spatial environment—it cannot be questioned politically.

In this perspective, it has also been made clear that real-space inequality can have many different faces, from gated communities to abstract atmospheres that have an excluding effect. Crucial to the evaluation of these inequalities is the distribution of resources that play a role in the socialisation and education process. Resources represent all material and immaterial means and circumstances that can facilitate an individual's social advancement, with the goal of improving one's position in society and participating in society's goods. At a first glance, this seems to imply the ubiquity of resources, as every place can in principle offer inspiration, contacts or individual support. The importance of habitus, which goes beyond occupational qualification and includes manners, style of dress, taste or language, seems to multiply the sources and places of acquisition in real space as well. At closer inspection, however, this diversity is also characterised by hierarchies and limitations. As has been illustrated, these hierarchies and limitations, together with the ongoing reproduction of unequal conditions produce a highly asymmetrical opportunity structure on a wide variety of scale levels that calls for an examination of all physical and perceived reference points of day-to-day life beyond the residential area, the school or the workplace. A more difficult or even non-existent access to places and persons offering relevant resources has been summarised in three mutually influencing dimensions: (a) physical inaccessibility and distance, (b) lack of perception and (c) social distance.

Because of its wealth of universally accessible resources, virtual space has the potential to overcome real-space limitations. Every user who is able to navigate cyberspace is given a new mobility that requires a reassessment of all three dimensions. In spite of the possibilities that cyberspace offers, it must not be forgotten that human action still requires physical space. Human activity aimed at fulfilling basic needs, as expressed systematically in the seven basic functions of existence (housing, work, consumption, education, recreation, use of infrastructure and living in community) (Partzsch 1970), does not have a counterpart in cyberspace. The place of residence with its functions for the body (shelter, sleep, food) remains a focus of daily life. Furthermore, it is not possible to learn and work entirely removed from real space, and both will also continue to require use of transportation in real space.

At the same time, for all basic functions of existence there are several examples of a partial real-space compensation which weaken the structure of real space and have an enabling quality resulting from the huge range of offers of the digital economy. For housing, it could be argued that location and furnishings partly lose their importance thanks to the options of obtaining numerous digital services. While a large *real-space distance* to relevant locations (ways of living alien to one's milieu, contact options, educational infrastructure) might persist, influencing the *perception* of valuable offers that exist outside of one's real-space world of daily life, cyberspace offers many alternatives. The variety of options provided by Internet-based services for ordinary needs and activities seems limitless. In the boundless expanse of the Internet, one can find countless offers to get to know content foreign to one´s own milieu and learn things that are relevant for upward mobility. Fundamentally, every user has access to a world promising contact and exchange via social networks, making products available through e-commerce or offering information in a variety of contexts. In the digital age, the simplified acquisition of global information and knowledge resources makes the place from which this takes place relative. In short, Bourdieu´s oft-cited "boundedness" no longer plays a role in the virtual context (Bourdieu 1991, S. 30; 1999, S. 127).

One of the basic functions of existence, *education*, which is the prerequisite for qualified work and a key factor in lowering inequality (cf. Piketty, 2014, p. 40), can be obtained by taking up and accepting the right virtual offers. Media literacy is of central importance here, its acquisition in school and everyday life providing new access to resources. The opportunities highlighted lie in the diversity of resources available via mobile phone or tablet, in new forms of teaching that weaken reproductive mechanisms in favour of technical skills, game-based approaches or group work, they lie in the individualisation of learning opportunities or in innovative programmes for the self-acquisition of knowledge (Choudhury et al. 2023).

Referring to Bourdieu and the practices of distinction detailed above, education requires not only school curricula, but also the possibility to get to know the relevant dimensions of taste and opinion which create distinction and demarcation in everyday life. Without doubt, the habitus continues to be shaped by the family as the traditional place of socialisation as well as by the larger social and spatial environment, and a person´s inner and outer reality are developed primarily in real space. Nevertheless, cyberspace always offers the chance to at least perceive content foreign to the milieu and even become part of a new community. The limitations of real space can be overcome by frequenting virtual facilities and online communities—at all times and in all places. Finding out about the latest trends in the virtual sphere does not require a day trip to the nearest metropolis. Museums make their content available online, and innovative computer games engage users with the experience of the unfamiliar. The exchange about trends, the display of taste and the articulation of social currents takes place on the open stage of streaming platforms, promotional videos, forums and networks. Real-space barriers and distances that contributed to a reproductive logic of stratification (club effects) are countered in cyberspace by universal accessibility.

Social network services in particular can be viewed as new virtual social spaces which, within the framework of the provider's fixed terms of use, serve every user's relationship and information management (Koput 2010; Schmidt et al. 2009, S. 27). While Bourdieu stressed the logic of the constitution of groups based on internal exchange and mutual recognition, contributing to the consolidation of group boundaries (Bourdieu 1983, S. 192), in cyberspace membership can be achieved after a few clicks. Now users can share their messages with everyone, express their interests in specialised communities, exchange ideas and join other groups at any time. Thereby, social spaces are not only pluralised, but they can overlap. Due to its size and diversity of use, Facebook is the ideal platform for studying how contacts are created and maintained. It allows one to look at other people's profiles, to leave messages there, to collect "friends" or to join groups with shared interests. As demonstrated by the study on adolescents' media activity conducted by Brüggen and Schemmerling (2014) with respect to Facebook, virtual social spaces are basically permeable. It is easy to make a first casual contact. In contrast, the study also found that the adolescents rarely make deliberate connections between different social spaces and in most cases, users interact with friends or friends of their friends. While in practice people do not necessarily connect with groups foreign to their own milieu, the technological conditions to do so do exist. Besides the access to cultural capital, network services also offer access to social capital. Numerous studies have been conducted drawing attention to the potential Facebook has in this respect. Relationships on social networks can strengthen real-space contact and help rekindle offline relationships from the past (Ellison et al. 2007; Subrahmanyam et al. 2008). Other studies have stressed how teenagers build relationships in the digital sphere (Manago et al. 2012), underscoring the positive correlation between the acquisition of social capital and the number of online friends as well as the time invested (Ellison et al. 2011; Steinfield et al. 2008). More recent investigations of the acquisition of social capital put a stronger emphasis on the way people act on the network. Intensive use of digital channels, it is shown, does not automatically lead to capital gains. It could be demonstrated that it takes more targeted messages to significantly improve individual consent (Bohn et al. 2014) or that introverted behaviour can seriously impede the acquisition of social capital compared to extroverted users (Weiqin et al.

2016). Despite the different preconditions that users bring with them, the opportunity for a casual and partly anonymous appearance on the net can alleviate the burdens of face-to-face interaction. Socially anxious and shy people seem to find it easier to express themselves and come into contact with others (Ellison et al. 2007), which can lead to positive self-effects (Valkenburg 2017).

In relation to resource access, these new conditions of making contact on Facebook and many other networks refer mainly to social distance in real space, where barriers exist even though the resources can be perceived and are within reach. This inability to fulfil implicit expectations, the problem of feeling out of place and not having the necessary capital, was the main focus of the works of Bourdieu. (cf. Bourdieu 1991, S. 32). As ascriptive characteristics (gender, appearance, clothes) do not really play a role in cyberspace, structures which in real space immediately lead to a milieu-specific pre-categorisation seem to lose their importance. The "subtle differences" in appearance, the refined codes in the choice of clothing or references associated with a self-designed living space—they all temporarily lose their importance in the virtual sphere. Some sensory impressions, such as smell or touch, play no role at all in digital interactions, and this is also true in part for auditory and visual expressions (cf. Suler 2015, S. 112ff). Across the spectrum of different communication channels, it is up to the user to decide which characteristics they want to hide at first and which ones they want to highlight. One could, therefore, argue that a *partial concealment of the habitus* gives one the possibility to acquire new resources in cyberspace. In addition, this opens up possibilities for an alternative self-definition. It is a free play of identities where new worlds of experience open up, bringing each user a bit closer to fulfilling their desire to choose their role. In her extensive studies about "Life on the Screen", Sherry Turkle captured in great detail the strategies and effects of the "newly chosen self" in qualitative interviews (Turkle 1998, S. 289ff). The chance to be whoever or whatever we want to be, experiment, act out fantasies, put on a disguise—they all severely undermine Bourdieu´s distinction mechanisms. While the effects of socialisation still exist, they can be expanded or concealed in a playful manner. As an expert in a community of one´s own choosing, a specialised blogger or anonymous activist, one can shed stereotypical categorisations about them, strategically putting the focus on strengths and interests. From a psychological perspective as well, it has been demonstrated how digital interaction detached from copresence influences personality and identity (cf. Renner et al. 2005).

In the meantime, offers on the Internet and in cyberspace have increased to such an extent that the chance to partly conceal the habitus, selectively highlighting available forms of capital, also works for other forms of social interaction: A virtual town hall, telemedical consultation, Internet banking or online shops deprive authorities, doctors, lenders or businesses of a lot of information they might have used to the client´s disadvantage in the pre-digital age. In addition, there other alternatives liberating users from constricting conventions, such as anonymous chats or self-chosen roles in virtual reality. Search engines, first and foremost Google, guide users toward their interests free of charge.

With regard to the basic function of existence "living in community", matchmaking agencies and dating apps could be mentioned, which at first also undermine negative pre-categorisations. The logic of likely contacts in the real-space environment of home, school or work as well as acquaintances from the familiar milieu is undermined in cyberspace. Finally, encounters can occur between people who would never have met in real space due to different action spaces, a lack of awareness of these spaces and of the possibility of social connection.

Finally, the basic functions of existence "participating in infrastructure" or "recreation" could, implemented in the virtual sphere, also make it possible to overcome the three restricting dimensions. While the opportunity to overcome spatial distances as a central characteristic of cyberspace has already been pointed out, this is only partially true for recreation, as in a vacation far from home. On the one hand, the digital possibilities of exploring far-away places (e.g., Google Earth, Bing Maps) and conditions (e.g., travel blogs, evaluation portals) can help to broaden one´s horizon. Seeing how others live, how they spend their free time and what their milieu looks like makes partial access possible, but this is certainly not the same as going somewhere for recreation (or for inspiration and education). What is more, it greatly depends on the available capital. At the same time, digital technologies make travel easier through price comparisons, and the quality of the stay can be improved. A smartphone with Internet access can be a valuable travel companion for everyone, independent of the social background. As demonstrated in studies by Wang et al. (2012, 2016), tourists feel safer thanks to the use of smartphones and are encouraged to explore more places and try out new things.

In summary, a look at the different basic functions of existence demonstrates that there are digital applications for all relevant areas of life that can build a bridge to resources relevant for social advancement. The example of the central square which has lost its agora function due to power-based arrangements and mechanisms of exclusions was used to illustrate the reproducing logic of stratification in real space. It seems that in the age of digitalisation; numerous new virtual squares are opening up that are accessible independent of one´s capital endowment. Neither inaccessibility nor distance nor perception or social distance are relevant dimensions of resource deprivation in cyberspace. Rather, the virtual sphere seems to offer the opportunity to acquire capital alternatively through education, contacts, information or creative forms of access.

However, the virtual sphere is usually not yet sufficient for their "valorisation" in the process of social advancement. The acquired social and cultural capital is still preliminary to the extent that it needs to prove itself in real space. After meeting a new partner through the Internet, it still needs to be determined if they are compatible in real life, and an applicant for a job or an apartment still has to face a personal interview. By the same token, virtual places cannot take over all functions of the public real space. Yet it cannot be denied that favourable preconditions for a successful date in the central square mentioned or a positive job interview at the office of a potential new employer can be created in the virtual sphere.

The ability to use the illustrated technological possibilities successfully is a sine qua non for capital acquisition. That means that in addition to the question of the convertibility of resources obtained in cyberspace, another limitation comes into play, bringing back the habitus through the back door.

3.3 Digital Divides, Inequalities and Digital Habitus

The term digital divides refers to inequality in terms of access to information and communication technologies as well as the ability to use them. In the recent past, the term digital inequalities has also come into use: From a global perspective, there are considerable differences in development, with many regions having neither the infrastructure nor enough end devices to enable people to participate in digitalisation at all. The technologically isolated sections of the population are at a disadvantage, and in an interconnected world economy this can affect their overall development opportunities as the gap between well-equipped and poorly equipped regions keeps getting wider (global divide). At a smaller scale, contrasts between urban and rural areas, differences in the speed of transmission, Wi-Fi density as well as politically motivated access restrictions can be identified. Finally, the quality of access to information and communication technologies must also be classified in the context of social and economic expectations.

But in the age of digitalisation, these inequalities regarding the access to technology and their far-reaching effects on the socially and digitally disadvantaged represent only one aspect of a structural disadvantage. A "second" digital divide becomes apparent when we look at the different abilities to use the available technologies. According to various studies, there are basic usage limitations and inequalities in terms of age, gender, ethnicity, health impairments and disabilities or due to different personality types (see DiMaggio et al. 2001, p. 311ff; Robinson et al. 2003, p. 17; Van Dijk 2014, p. 60). More specifically, when it comes to a capital-enhancing use of the new communication and information technologies, especially Internet use, we are again faced with the problem of social inequality, as the corresponding competencies are tied to a person's social background. Statistically, there are clear correlations: The higher the educational level, the higher the level of Internet literacy and the more varied, differentiated and critical the use of digitally transmitted information will be (Kammer 2014, p. 99ff; Zillien 2009; van Dijk 2020).

This second level of digital inequality becomes all the more apparent as differences in availability hardly exist anymore in affluent service societies. This is also the case in Germany, where user devices are now almost ubiquitous, regardless of social milieus and educational backgrounds (MPFS, 2019, p. 5ff). With regard to the socio-spatial influence on socialisation, we therefore need to investigate in more detail to what extent the freedom to break out of one's own milieu with the help of technology is lost again due to a lack of knowledge and interest. Ultimately, we can only speak of "digital inclusion" if the unequal conditions of real space do not spill over into the virtual sphere. In fact, it is precisely these limitations of real space that are expressed in the numerous studies on young people's media usage. While young people from educated milieus demonstrate a bigger interest in the Internet as a source of knowledge and information as well as a greater ability to search for information in a targeted manner, those with a lower level of education also show a significantly lower degree of mastery in their use of the Internet (Hatlevik and Christophersen 2013; Iske et al. 2005; Otto et al. 2005). A person's educational background also influences the use of video platforms, and young people with a lower level of education are more likely to use media in a consumerist and uncritical way. The same applies to the use of search engines to look for information (Hargittai and Hinnant 2008; Iske et al. 2007, p. 78) or profitable participation in e-commerce (Buhtz et al. 2014).

The great significance of the differences in use has to do also with the developmental stage of the adolescent subjects: The increased use of media in late childhood and especially in adolescence coincides with an important stage of socialisation in which the aim is to build up a stable ego identity and become a full member of society. In the conflict between personal individuation and social integration, the challenging task is to develop a stable inner system in face of the numerous demands for action and offers of everyday life. In this context, the possibilities of cyberspace as described above provide numerous templates, while also presupposing a certain ability to decide what is relevant amidst diverse and contradictory content (Hurrelmann and Bauer 2018, p. 83ff).

From the perspective of society as a whole, a correlation between education, social class and Internet use can also be identified. A large majority of users with little familiarity with the Internet comes from disadvantaged milieus (e.g., DIVSI 2016). The similarity of the Internet milieus to the well-known Sinus milieus (which correlate basic social views and orientations with the social milieu) suggests that social strata and basic attitudes are carried over from the offline to the online world.

There is another reason why the vision of an expanded freedom of action in cyberspace has its limits: The individual's own conditioning also accompanies the particular *types of action* in the virtual world (interaction with others, selection of topics, setting of preferences, etc.) as well as the perception of the resources to be acquired. Since media usage is always based on existing interests and abilities, a more precise differentiation of the various motives and contents in virtual space is necessary. Beyond important capabilities such as literacy, language skills, prior knowledge and the capacity for critical reflection, it is evident that the demand for and communication about available content, forums and networks in cyberspace differ across social milieus (Biermann 2009; Ragnedda and Ruiu 2018). It is the dispositions acquired in real space that also guide users in the digital sphere. The habitus becomes the "digital habitus".

The transfer of unequal social conditions into cyberspace can again be studied by looking at the use of social networks. The opportunity for new self-presentation through the profile, including the choice of a photo, which Ellison et al. praised as a "social lubricant" for establishing contact (2011, p. 887f), can only help to reach people outside of one's own milieu if it corresponds to their interests and tastes. Being able to maintain old contacts, expressing interest and receiving responses and successfully participating in topic-related communities—none of these things automatically mean that one is able to obtain resources that are relevant for upward mobility. Rather, the digital habitus relegates users to those contacts and contents that have already been part of their development in the real-space socialisation process. Indeed, it has been demonstrated that habitualised usage practices in cyberspace reflect milieu affiliations and patterns of virtual appropriation are associated with processes of distinction (Boyd, 2014; Lambert, 2016; Meyen, 2007; Witzel 2012; Yates and Lockley, 2018).

In contrast to the opportunities that were postulated with the virtual elimination of real-space limitations, these studies show that the beneficiaries of the digital age can be found among the already privileged: A high capital budget results in increased capital accumulation in cyberspace. The fact that the educated and wealthier segments of the population profit more can be interpreted as a growing distancing from the socially and economically disadvantaged segments of the population, exposing the Internet as a tool of social stratification. Massimo Ragnedda identifies this logic of reproduction as a third digital divide, resulting from the unequal social gains of Internet use (2017, p. 76).

It would be premature, however, to dismiss the new possibilities for action that cyberspace and the Internet offer because of these unequal returns on use. *For one thing*, in the context of a comprehensive digitalisation, the information and communications revolution must be viewed as a framework for society as a whole, which includes the attempt to find solutions to the social question. As digital technologies gradually penetrate all areas of life, a change is under way that will eventually affect everyone in society, forcing us to come to terms with the new conditions. The failure to look at the options involved is tantamount to giving a relative advantage to those segments of the population that use the technology.

Second, regarding the opportunity for social advancement of capital-poor milieus, the digital divides do not mean that the opportunities for acquiring capital in cyberspace no longer exist. Compared to the stratifying mechanisms in real space, cyberspace remains a sphere of high accessibility, clearly different from the fixed socialisation context with its social and physical realities. The possibility to use it in the process of capital acquisition is facilitated by the option to strategically conceal the habitus in order to prevent negative distinction practices and be able to practice one's own distinction. The fact that access to these options always depends on the resources available (second digital divide) and that these can have a reproductive effect (third digital divide) does not put the options themselves into question. It is rather an issue of how the automatic transition from the habitus shaped by real space mitigated if the former implies disadvantages.

Thirdly, it must therefore by no means be assumed that overcoming these divides is impossible. Ideally, resource acquisition in cyberspace requires motivated and informed users who know how to navigate the digital sphere. What is needed is the potential to reflect, so that exclusionary processes of distinction in cyberspace are recognised, and a corresponding awareness, so that milieu-induced self-exclusion does not stand in the way of advancement from the outset. Against this background, research in the fields of media pedagogy and education increasingly focuses on measures that could offer disadvantaged adolescents development opportunities beyond their milieu of origin (Ragnetta 2017, p. 91ff; Van Dijk 2014, p. 113ff).

3.4 Interim Conclusion: The Digital Acquisition of Opportunities?

Increasing the value of cyberspace with the help of new sources of information and contact, new offers of access and perception could help overcome the limitations of real space which have effectively and reflectively constricted the socially disadvantaged segments of the population. Beyond the usual residential environment, there is the possibility to relate to geographically distant places, anonymous forms of communication diminish the importance of cultural capital and sources of knowledge acquisition multiply. In this way, the Internet and the mobile usage devices associated with it (cell phones, tablets), as well as other gateways to cyberspace take on enormous relevance for socialisation and education. With the help of virtual contacts, the immediate physical environment can be enriched and even skipped. Reproductive institutions of the neighbourhood tend to lose their social significance.

Conversely, managing this new-gained freedom and being able to access information on the Internet at will also means that obtaining these options depends on the user´s interests and skills. For the capital-poor segments of the population, this carries the danger of the habitus once more negatively impacting the individual's acquisition of resources, as that which has been acquired in the real world will rub off on the digital habitus. In the context of digital inequalities, digital space must by no means be viewed as an egalitarian alternative space, as inequality is perpetuated in it. Accordingly, academic research focuses on individuals´ restrictions of action, which are believed to reside primarily in users´ lack of skills, online as well as offline. In this respect, media literacy means the ability to make use of the variety of resources already available. The deprivation of opportunities in real space illustrated above could be counteracted with a "digital acquisition of opportunities".

What is surprising is that this widespread academic focus on user skills ignores the possibility that resource acquisition may also be systemically constrained by the provider.

In comparison with real space, which is constituted by actions, cyberspace is characterised by a far-reaching predefinition of what actions are basically possible. As has been illustrated by reference to programmed codes and their significance, space-constituting practices can affect the system of cyberspace without the actors responsible for them (programmers, financiers, etc.) acting within this system. In the virtual world, they create framework conditions for the actions of others, conditions which they themselves are independent of. In contrast, the actors in real space can also be located in this space and are subject to the social and spatial structures of this system (Löw 2016, p. 145f). Arrangement and spacing in real space is possible only under the rules and resources that exist there, exerting recursive influence primarily in these contexts (disregarding, for the time being, mixed forms due to the partial digital penetration of real space) (cf. Ibid., p. 141).

With the separation into two separate spheres, the recursivity as well as the "duality of space" cease to exist. Those who constitute the spaces of digital platforms, games or social networks have a high degree of freedom and great power, since they are, as it were, outside the system, intangible even for users.

As the focus mostly lies on accessibility, individual benefit and the fact that it is free of charge, this power is hardly ever questioned. In the context of socialisation and education, cyberspace is perceived as offering numerous options, and with the help of certain skills that still need to be promoted the right contents or contacts can be selected. Although the largest and most heavily used part of cyberspace is provided by commercial operators, the costs of using the available content are hardly ever mentioned. In fact, payment consists in the data-based registration of all activities. As will be shown in the next section, the collection of this user data leads to a highly unequal and recursive use of digital offerings, which means that the opportunity for social advancement ultimately means much more than overcoming the aforementioned divides.

References

Biermann, Ralf (2009): Die Bedeutung des Habitus-Konzepts für die Erforschung soziokultureller Unterschiede im Bereich der Medienpädagogik. *MedienPädagogik* 17, 1–18.

Bohn, Angela; Buchta, Christian; Hornik, Kurt & Mair, Patrick (2014): Making Friends and Communicating on Facebook: Implications for the Access to Social Capital. *Social Networks* 37, 29–41.

Bourdieu, Pierre (1979): *Entwurf einer Theorie der Praxis auf der ethnologischen Grundlage der Kabylischen Gesellschaft*. Frankfurt a. M.: Suhrkamp.

Bourdieu, Pierre (1983): Ökonomisches Kapital, kulturelles Kapital, soziales Kapital. In: Reinhard Kreckel (Hrsg.): Soziale Ungleichheiten. Göttingen: Schwartz, S. 183–198.

Bourdieu, Pierre (1991): Physischer, sozialer und angeeigneter physischer Raum. In: Martin Wentz (Hrsg.): *Stadt-Räume*. Frankfurt a. M.: Campus Verlag, 25–34.

Bourdieu, Pierre (1999): *The Weight of the World: Social Suffering in Contemporary* Society. Stanford, CA.: Stanford University Press.

Boyd, Danah (2014): *Es ist kompliziert. Das Leben der Teenager in sozialen Netzwerken*. München: Redline Verlag.

Brüggen, Nils & Schemmerling, Mareike (2014): Das Social Web und die Aneignung von Sozialräumen. Forschungsperspektiven auf das sozialraumbezogene Medienhandeln von Jugendlichen in Sozialen Netzwerkdiensten. In: *sozialraum.de* 6 (1). Online: https://www.sozialraum.de/das-social-web-und-die-aneignung-von-sozialraeumen.php (01.03.2023)

Buhtz, Katharina; Reinartz, Annika; Koenig, Andreas; Graf-Vlachy, Lorenz & Mammen, Jan (2014): Second-Order Digital Inequality: The Case of

E-Commerce. *International Conference on Information Systems*. Online: https://ssrn.com/abstract=2876126. (01.03.2023)

Choudhury, Amitava; Biswas, Arindam & Chakraborti, Sadhan (eds.) (2023): *Digital Learning Based Education Transcending Physical Barriers*. Singapore: Springer Nature.

Deutsches Institut für Vertrauen und Sicherheit im Internet (DIVSI) (2016): DIVSI Internet-Milieus 2016. Die digitalisierte Gesellschaft in Bewegung. Hamburg. Online: https://www.divsi.de/publikationen/studien/divsi-internet-milieus-2016-die-digitalisierte-gesellschaft-bewegung/index.html (01.03.2023)

DiMaggio, Paul; Hargittai, Eszter; Neuman, Russell W. & Robinson, John P. (2001): Social Implications of the Internet. *Annual. Review of Sociology* 27, S307–336.

Ellison, Nicole B.; Steinfield, Charles & Lampe, Cliff (2007): The Benefits of Facebook 'Friends': Exploring the Relationship Between College Students' Use of Online Social Networks and Social Capital. *Journal of Computer-mediated Communication* 12, 1143–1168.

Ellison, Nicole B.; Steinfield, Charles & Lampe, Cliff (2011): Connection Strategies: Social Capital Implications of Facebook-enabled Communication Practices. *New Media & Society* 13 (6), 873–892.

Hahn, Kornelia (2021): *Social Digitalisation: Persistent Transformations Beyond Digital Technology*. Cham: Palgrave Macmillan.

Hargittai, Eszter & Hinnant, Amanda (2008): Digital Inequality. *Communication Research* 35 (5), 602–621.

Hatlevik, Ove Edvard & Christophersen, Knut-Andreas (2013): Digital Competence at the Beginning of Upper Secondary School: Identifying Factors Explaining Digital Inclusion. *Computers & Education* 63, 240–247.

Herrmann, Heike (2010): Raumbegriffe und Forschungen zum Raum—eine Einleitung. In: Heike Herrmann (ed.): *RaumErleben. Zur Wahrnehmung des Raumes in Wissenschaft und Praxis*. Opladen: Budrich, 7–30.

Housley, William; Edwards, Adam; Beneito-Montagut, Roser & Fitzgerald, Richard (eds.) (2022): *The SAGE Handbook of Digital Society*. Los Angeles, London, New Delhi: Sage.

Hurrelmann, Klaus & Bauer, Ullrich (2018): *Socialisation During the Life Course*. New York, London: Routledge.

Iske, Stefan; Klein, Alex; Kutscher, Nadia & Otto, Hans-Uwe (2007): Virtuelle Ungleichheit und informelle Bildung: eine empirische Analyse der Internnutzung Jugendlicher und ihre Bedeutung für Bildung und gesellschaftliche Teilhabe. In: Hans-Uwe Otto (ed.): *Grenzenlose Cyberwelt? Zum Verhältnis von digitaler Ungleichheit und neuen Bildungszugängen für Jugendliche*. Wiesbaden: Springer VS, 65–92.

Iske, Stefan; Klein, Alexandra & Kutscher, Nadia (2005): Differences in Internet Usage—Social Inequality and Informal Education. *Social Work & Society* 3 (2), 215–223.
Kammer, Matthias (2014): *Kinder, Jugendliche und junge Erwachsene in der digitalen Welt. Eine Grundlagenstudie des SINUS-Instituts Heidelberg und des Deutschen Instituts für Vertrauen und Sicherheit im Internet* (DIVSI). Hamburg.
Kitchin, Rob & Dodge, Martin (2011): *Code/Space: Software and Everyday Life*. Cambridge: MIT Press.
Koput, Kenneth (2010): *Social Capital an Introduction to Managing Networks*. Northampton, Mass, Edward Elgar.
Lambert, Alex (2016): Intimacy and Social Capital on Facebook: Beyond the Psychological Perspective. *New Media & Society* 18 (11), 2559–2575.
Löw, Martina (2016): *The Sociology of Space: Materiality, Social Structures, and Action*. New York: Palgrave Macmillan.
Manago, Adriana M.; Taylor, Tamara & Greenfield, Patricia M. (2012): Me and my 400 friends: The Anatomy of College Students' Facebook Networks, their Communication Patterns, and well-being. *Developmental psychology* 48 (2), 369–380.
Meyen, Michael (2007): Medienwissen und Medienmenüs als kulturelles Kapital und als Distinktionsmerkmale. Eine Typologie der Mediennutzer in Deutschland. *Medien & Kommunikationswissenschaft* 55 (3), 333–354.
Mitchell, William J. (1996): *City of Bits. Space, Place, and the Infobahn*. Cambridge: MIT Press.
MPFS (ed.) (2019): JIM-Studie 2019. Jugend. Information. Medien. Stuttgart. Online: https://www.mpfs.de/fileadmin/files/Studien/JIM/2019/JIM_2019.pdf (01.03.2023)
Negroponte, Nicolas (1995): *Total Digital—Die Welt zwischen 0 und 1 oder: Die Zukunft der Kommunikation*. München: Goldmann.
Otto, Hans-Uwe; Kutscher, Nadia; Klein, Alexandra & Iske, Stefan (2005): *Soziale Ungleichheit im virtuellen Raum: Wie nutzen Jugendliche das Internet? Erste Ergebnisse einer empirischen Untersuchung zu Online-Nutzungsdifferenzen und Aneignungsstrukturen von Jugendlichen*. Berlin.
Partzsch, Dieter (1970): *Handwörterbuch der Raumforschung + Raumordnung*. Hannover: Jänecke.
Piketty, Thomas (2014): *Capital in the Twenty-First Century*. Cambridge: Harvard University Press.
Ragnedda, Massimo & Ruiu, Maria Laura (2018): Social Capital and the Three Levels of Digital Divide. In: Ibid. & Glenn W. Muschert (eds.): *Theorizing Digital Divides*. Milton: Routledge, 21–34.
Ragnedda, Massimo (2017): *The Third Digital Divide. A Weberian Approach to Digital Inequalities*. New York: Routledge.

Renner, Karl-Heinz; Schütz, Astrid & Machilek, Franz (eds.) (2005): *Internet und Persönlichkeit. Differentiell-psychologische und diagnostische Aspekte der Internetnutzung.* Göttingen: Hogrefe Verlag.

Rheingold, Howard (1994): *Virtuelle Gemeinschaft: soziale Beziehungen im Zeitalter des Computers.* Boston: Addison-Wesley.

Robinson, John P.; DiMaggio, Paul & Hargittai, Eszter (2003): New Social Survey Perspectives on the Digital Divide. *IT & Society* 1 (5), 1–22.

Schmidt, Jan Hinrik; Paus-Hasebrink, Ingrid & Hasebrink, Uwe (eds.) (2009): *Heranwachsen mit dem Social Web. Zur Rolle von Web 2.0-Angeboten im Alltag von Jugendlichen und jungen Erwachsenen.* Berlin: Vistas-Verlag.

Steinfield, Charles; Ellison, Nicole B. & Lampe, Cliff (2008): Social Capital, Self-esteem, and Use of Online Social Network Sites: A Longitudinal Analysis. *Journal of Applied Developmental Psychology* 29 (6), 434–445.

Subrahmanyam, Kaveri; Reich, Stephanie M.; Waechter, Natalia & Espinoza, Guadalupe (2008): Online and Offline Social Networks: Use of Social Networking Sites by Emerging Adults. *Journal of Applied Developmental Psychology* 29 (6), 420–433.

Suler, John, R. (2015): *Psychology of the Digital Age. Humans become electric.* Cambridge: Cambridge University Press.

Thiedeke, Udo (ed.) (2004): *Soziologie des Cyberspace. Medien, Strukturen und Semantiken.* Wiesbaden: Springer VS.

Turkle, Sherry (1998): *Leben im Netz. Identität in Zeiten des Internet.* Reinbek bei Hamburg: Rowohlt.

Valkenburg, Patti M. (2017): Understanding Self-Effects in Social Media. *Human Communication Research* 43 (4), 477–490.

Van Dijk, Jan A.G.M (2020): *The Digital Divide.* Cambridge: Polity Press.

Van Dijk, Jan A.G.M. (2014): The Evolution of the Digital Divide: The Digital Divide Turns to Inequality of Skills and Usage. *New Media & Society* 16 (3), S. 507–526.

Wang, Dan; Park, Sangwon & Fesenmaier, Daniel R. (2012): The Role of Smartphones in Mediating the Touristic Experience. *Journal of Travel Research* 51 (4), 371–387.

Wang, Dan; Xiang, Zheng & Fesenmaier, Daniel R. (2016): Smartphone Use in Everyday Life and Travel. *Journal of Travel Research* 55 (1), 52–63.

Weiqin, Eliza Leong; Campbell, Marilyn; Kimpton, Melanie; Wozencroft, Kelly & Orel, Alexandra (2016): Social Capital on Facebook. *Journal of Educational Computing Research* 54 (6), 747–786.

Witzel, Marc (2012): Medienhandeln, digitale Ungleichheit und Distinktion. *Merz—Zeitschrift für Medienpädagogik* (6), 81–92.

Yates, Simeon & Lockley, Eleanor (2018): Social Media and Social Class. *American Behavioral Scientist* 62 (9), 1291–1316.

Zillien, Nicole (2009): *Digitale Ungleichheit. Neue Technologien und alte Ungleichheiten in der Informations- und Wissensgesellschaft*. Wiesbaden: Springer VS.

Zook, Matthew & Graham, Mark (2018): Hacking Code/Space: Confounding the Code of Global Capitalism. *Transactions of the Institute of British Geographers* 42, 1–15.

Open Access This chapter is licensed under the terms of the Creative Commons Attribution 4.0 International License (http://creativecommons.org/licenses/by/4.0/), which permits use, sharing, adaptation, distribution and reproduction in any medium or format, as long as you give appropriate credit to the original author(s) and the source, provide a link to the Creative Commons license and indicate if changes were made.

The images or other third party material in this chapter are included in the chapter's Creative Commons license, unless indicated otherwise in a credit line to the material. If material is not included in the chapter's Creative Commons license and your intended use is not permitted by statutory regulation or exceeds the permitted use, you will need to obtain permission directly from the copyright holder.

CHAPTER 4

Data-Based Utilisation Contexts

Abstract Personalised data are used in different economic contexts of utilisation to target users with the right products, information and services. The channels through which person-related data are obtained are as various as the possibilities of approaching people individually. While the extensive knowledge about users provides the topic for research looking into (government) surveillance or the loss of privacy, this chapter focuses on the significance of self-mirroring: What are the social implications of targeting every user individually when people are confronted with the economic expression of their own dispositions? Numerous examples will illustrate that such a recursive reference is possible and widely used for the majority of day-to-day activities, online as well as offline.

Keywords Data economy · Digital marketing · Filter bubble · Personal data · Mirrored spaces

Virtually all of the numerous publications on the new possibilities of computer-aided data analysis refer to it as a revolution. A revolution that, following the spread of the PC and the internet, has new and far-reaching consequences for the digitalisation of everyday life. The exponential growth in data sets that can no longer be analysed using conventional methods is referred to as big data (Hilbert and López 2011). Currently, it takes less than two years for the global data volume to double. This unrestrained growth is likely to continue in the future, with the development of the Internet of Things, data from social networks, the growing number of sensors in smartphones, cameras in all places, GPS-based motion profiles or radio waves that contribute to contactless identification (RFID), intelligent clothing and many other data sources.

Yet the revolution that is talked about in relation to big data does not refer to a supposedly uncontrollable flood of data, but rather to the technological possibility of using these data as a valuable resource. The goal is therefore to collect even more of them. Thanks to increasing computing power, innovative techniques of data acquisition and ever more intelligent algorithms in the evaluation software, they promise companies, organisations, politicians and private users enormous gains in knowledge in many different fields of activity. It is becoming increasingly possible to identify relationships that were previously too complex for human capacities, using them to develop models that deliver valid predictions for future behaviour. Scholars have been talking about the end of theory, as the abundance of data allows almost any correlation to be calculated without making assumptions, and the data-based competition between companies for customers it will lead to is referred to as "digital Darwinism" (Kreutzer and Land 2015). In another context, the data revolution creates the possibility of total surveillance of one's own body, turning sick people into medical professionals and hospitals into globally oriented databases (Herland et al. 2014). Urban planners are envisioning future "smart cities" where energy and transportation flows, utilities and social communications are linked into a comprehensive control system (Dameri and Rosenthal-Sabroux 2014). In the economic realm, the consequences of increasingly autonomous, data-driven decision-making processes (Power 2015) as well as the prospects of a healthcare system permanently interlinked with humans (Khoury and Ioannidis, 2014) are discussed.

This revolution marks a fundamental expansion of cyberspace, allowing for networked miniature computers to intrude into the real-space everyday environment. In cities in particular, this is happening so naturally that users of smart homes or customers facing the advertising on their display that reacts autonomously are less and less aware of the space in which they are acting in any given moment. Cyberspace and physical real space are fused in ways that are slowly transforming physical space into digitalised space.

In relation to the debate on social inequality (and considering the limitations that have been discussed), the ubiquity of data mediated by computers could improve opportunities for advancement, as they imply a further spread of digital modes. Resources relevant to advancement, such as information and contacts, are becoming even easier to obtain, and with them opportunities for utilisation and qualification.

But releasing data is not all the digitalised economy is doing. It is also recording them, utilising personal data with maximum efficiency. Personal data generally refers to information about an identified or identifiable natural person. The possibility of obtaining personal data is firmly embedded in ambient intelligence, both online and offline, and must therefore be considered as a general condition for digitally enhanced modes of action.

As will be shown, private-sector data utilisation in particular can be accompanied by highly specific influences with a stratifying effect both in real space and in virtual space. In this context, too, we are dealing with a revolution that is taking place slowly and quietly, but which will massively restrict the opportunities for advancement of disadvantaged segments of the population in the long term.

This section will look at the utilisation contexts in the data-related value creation process, based on the sources that are used for generating personal data. Looking at actors such as data traders and companies, who will not be able to compete without customer data in the future, the techniques of influencing individuals in cyberspace and digitalised real space will be presented, followed by an analysis of the socially stratifying effects of big data.

4.1 Personalised Data and Their New Sources

In all of our daily activities, we leave data traces. Starting with the name on the birth certificate, the accumulation of personal data continues with the application for official documents and the registration of a place of residence with a specific address. We shop at certain places, possibly paying with a debit card or perhaps even using a personalised loyalty card. We sign credit and insurance contracts, participate in surveys and contests or book a vacation. In the virtual sphere, we communicate on social networks, take an interest in certain news, use search engines and shop online according to our individual preferences. In each of these situations, personal data are generated.

While the storage of basic data by public authorities beyond a certain scope has repeatedly been the subject of critical debate (census, data retention), public awareness of the private-sector's interest in personal data has only developed more recently. Meanwhile, for many private-sector businesses, capturing the everyday routines of individuals via their real-space and digital traces has long been standard practice: Information from offline and online sources is collected, categorised and analysed. Big data enables companies to track each consumer individually according to their preferences and habits across all basic functions of existence by analysing consumption, search behaviour, sales, page views, geographic location, demographics, social situation or contacts with others. The methods and technologies used for this purpose can be summarised under the term data mining; a process where raw data are transformed into information that can be put into value in various ways.

Data mining is particularly important in the context of internet use. It is true that the possibilities of obtaining consumer data in physical space have increased notably in recent years, as postal addresses, vouchers or customer cards are evaluated via modern database management systems. But for all parties with a commercial interest, the steady online influx of data holds infinitely more potential, as IP addresses, personalised logins, the setting of cookies and other tracking methods have made it easy to follow individual traces on the internet. With the help of search queries, ratings, web browser information or biometric data, it has become possible to precisely identify individuals and systematically evaluate their online activities (cf. Bujlow et al. 2017).

The predominance of smartphones on the mobile device market provides particularly favourable conditions for personalised data analysis. Since a smartphone is usually only used by its owner and accompanies them permanently, the device contains many user specifics. Addresses and photos stored in it, active contacts, calendar entries, visited pages as well as extensive location data provide a wealth of information about its owner.

In addition, data that are collected from the digital networking of numerous everyday objects can measure individual actions and activities. Microcontrollers, i.e., small, powerful computers on chips, enable elements of the physical environment to communicate with each other and to process information in a personalised manner. Such connectivity goes far beyond the portable data storage devices (wearables) already mentioned and is increasingly permeating our everyday lives (Jin et al. 2018). For example, households can be equipped with remote-controlled heating, cooling or water supply systems, intelligent household appliances can be adjusted to the preferences of their owners, sensors can autonomously alert the police and fire department in the event of faults and medical care can be geared to regularly used measuring devices. Thanks to its cost and environmental efficiency, smart metering is becoming increasingly common in many households. To optimise energy consumption, data on the power consumption of each household is being recorded in real time. However, the data not only reveal the consumption curve over the course of the day, but also allow conclusions to be drawn about which devices are used and when. In this way, each household´s preferences and habits become transparent. Power consumption can be used to determine when people get up, and screen brightness can be used to determine which films are being watched (Cuijpers and Koops 2013).

The merging of objects from the physical world with their representation in the world of data to form hybrid systems is often seen as the new revolution of the internet. The Internet of Things implies a memorisation capability of objects to record, store and retrieve information. Furthermore, this information can also be processed in a context-dependent manner. It is significant that the availability of data for a particular object does not depend exclusively on external sources, such as information from smartphones or from external providers. In addition, many objects are able to use sensory capabilities to gather information on their own and interact with the environment. An extension of the Internet of Things to the residential and living areas of the urban population results in the concept of the smart city, that is, a data-driven urban development aimed at social, economic and technical innovations. While there are various ideas about what this concept looks like in concrete terms (Cocchia 2014 for an overview), a smart city involves finding solutions to current problems through the intelligent networking of urban space. Across the globe, the focus lies on infrastructure improvement, environmental protection, community participation, economic productivity and public utilities, with data-driven intelligence promising increased efficiency, performance and competitiveness. Another central component of the concept of the smart city is the digital measurement of social routines in urban space.

This digital penetration adds further complexity to the conceptualisation of space as a relational arrangement. In order to detect different structural features with regard to capital acquisition, physical real space and cyberspace were first compared with each other, taking into account reciprocal references and the option of simultaneous utilisation. Something as simple as a tweet in a pedestrian zone involves a double action in space: First, depending on its importance, it leads to changes in cyberspace that other Twitter users refer to. A transfer back to physical space can happen as soon as the tweet influences actions there (A more extreme example of this could be the crash of a stock price as a result of a tweet, which in turn would lead to capital withdrawal and altered conditions for action in numerous places around the world). At the same time, the tweeting user directly influences the constitution of the real space they are in through their presence.

With the digital networking of social goods and people, yet another structurally defining form of the digital now comes into play, resulting in an external predetermination of the conditions for action. With reference to the global interlinking of actions (the tweet causing repercussions across borders could again be mentioned here), the duality of space has been generalised to the extent that action results and action conditions can diverge spatially and agents can no longer be identified in a global constitution process. With digitalisation, however, the structure is not only (partly) shaped by external factors, but the external becomes an actual *part* of the structure. Social assets, as well as people themselves, can be linked to technology, data, messages and instructions. With smart implants, they can even merge into one unit. The power to constitute space no longer lies solely with those actors who act in real space under the rules that apply there, but to a significant extent it lies with those actors who control the code of the technologies used (Kitchin and Dodge 2011). The limitations to bring about a structural change in cyberspace described above therefore also characterise digitalised real space to an increasing extent. As has been explained with reference to cyberspace, the external predetermination of the digitally expanded framework of action does not seem to be accompanied by a limitation of individual possibilities at first. On the contrary, the countless offers of cyberspace and digitalised real spaces provide many additional options, their attractiveness constantly reaffirming the digital lifestyle. The surrender of specific rights, including personal data, is the only price to be paid.

From the point of view of data utilisation, digitalised real space, compared to virtual space, is characterised by a direct recording of personal characteristics. Routines and preferences are being transmitted directly and authentically, inviting a response in real space on the part of the public, but also on the part of commercial actors. The penetration of digital recording and processing capacities into the private sphere must be seen as a key prerequisite for corresponding data use, as has recently become possible and common through the acquisition of networked consumer products (such as cars, televisions, wearables or kitchen appliances).

The so-called sentient city—an urban space interspersed with sensors, cameras, actuators and data clouds and endowed with autonomous response and control capabilities—is already being examined as a social and political sphere for the future (Shepard 2011; Thrift 2014). The new conditions discussed with respect to this urban context are expressed in several ways (cf. Crang and Graham 2007): On the one hand, the sentient city implies an extension of real space by overlaying physical objects with virtual objects. The conventional topography of the city gives way to a personalised environment that can affect the individual in real time. Signs, ads and physical access points in urban spaces change depending on the individual identified. On the other hand, humans actively transfer functions to the environment via various technical aids surrounding them, creating an environment that is an expression of delegated functions and interests (Amoore and Piotukh 2016). Expanding this perspective, we could envision algorithms that automatically bring together people, places and objects (Safransky 2020). With the growing ability of computers to learn autonomously, i.e., the development of artificial intelligence, correlations between cause and effect, action and reaction are no longer trackable.

Such spacing (here more in the sense of "positioning" as opposed to "erecting") takes place largely unnoticed, as spaces are marked and occupied mostly without physical change. The corresponding technical conditions are visually inconspicuous, the data and working algorithms as invisible as their creators (Greenspan 2021). In contrast, when the positioning of people changes, the constitution of space does happen noticeably. Its composition and the atmosphere that changes with it then shape perception and the operation of synthesis in a way that clearly offers the capital-poor segments of the population fewer opportunities for connection (Eubanks 2018).

However the sentient city will look in the coming decades in technical and social terms, at present the diversity of data sources is already evident, as is their potential for selective exploitation. This is also underscored by a thriving data market that is nurtured by professional data traders and absorbed by enterprises.

4.2 An Efficient Form of Address: On the Utilisation of Personal Data

The private-sector exploitation of data is shared by companies that have their own online and offline data collection capacities or generate data themselves by offering internet services, by specialised service providers that extract data from the internet and process it for third parties and by data traders who specialise in selling data. All three groups also act as buyers in data markets. A clear distinction between them is not practicable, since the service packages of many providers include both the collection and the processing and trading of data. With the help of various analysis tools, even small companies outside the field can become players in the international data business.

Every form of new, digitally-based gathering of information builds on a technical infrastructure that makes the systematic accumulation of data possible in the first place. Even if the actors involved in data processing and data trading have not created this technical infrastructure themselves, they are links in the complex chain of a data-based value creation process that ultimately helps to define the programming of codes as well as the setting of rules in cyberspace and in digitalised real space. The opportunity to monetise what can be captured digitally is having an impact on the technical orientation of many offerings. In business, personal data are paving the way for various applications, especially in the product areas of marketing, people search and risk protection.

Database marketing is generally understood as the development and use of customer databases to increase marketing productivity through more effective acquisition, retention and development of customers (Blattberg et al. 2008, p. 4). Closely related to database marketing are the concepts of direct marketing and dialog marketing. The term direct marketing describes all marketing activities that aim to address a target person and achieve a measurable reaction (response), with the goal of establishing long-term direct contact and maintain it as permanently as possible. Personal sales letters, e-mails, SMS, calls by call centres or even personal interaction with a representative ensure that direct contact with the customer or prospect can be established and that their reactions can be recorded and systematically evaluated in databases. The term dialog marketing, which has been used more in recent years than direct marketing, focuses on longer-term interaction with the target person. While direct and dialog marketing emphasise interaction with individual customers and potential prospects, which can be realised both via virtual and real-space channels, online marketing (also referred to as web marketing or internet marketing) focuses exclusively on communication channels on the internet. In addition to the provider's website, this includes various forms of online advertising (such as classic banner advertising). In addition, there are advertising messages contained in media sharing platforms (e.g., YouTube or Flickr), online stores and downstream e-mail advertising, as well as all measures that initiate visits to a specific website via search engines (search engine marketing) or via social networks (social media marketing). The strategic goal of providers here is to influence blogs in order to bring goods and services into the conversation. They closely follow online conversations (text mining), try to gain a foothold in forums and communities, influence word-of-mouth or post targeted messages on social media sites (Droste 2014; Dwyer 2009; Yadav et al. 2015).

Mobile marketing is another rapidly growing segment of online marketing. With the help of location-based services, messages and offers can be tailored to the user's particular location. This structuring of information around the user in real space will facilitate a highly personalised approach in the future. On smartphones, advertising can be displayed near the product, and with the help of augmented reality commercial offers can be presented based on previous consumption habits (O'Mahony 2015). For example, there are apps that help a consumer navigate through a supermarket based on their preferences (e.g., Millonig and Gartner, 2011). Expanding on this development from an economic perspective, environments will likely one day be designed in an individualised manner, focusing on marketability.

Many companies are attempting to verify the identity of individuals or validate the classification of people, accounts or products to minimise default risks and assess the basis of business interaction. The insurance and healthcare industries rely on the data traders' portfolio in the fight against manipulated billing and falsified applications, as do the financial services sector and internet mail order businesses in their fight against fraud attempts. A key measure in combating fraud is to quickly identify individuals and existing connections between individuals. Thanks to personalised data, many customers can be assigned a specific risk value that provides information about their liquidity and their reliability. In the area of creditworthiness, sophisticated scoring models have become established that convert a large number of different life data into the probability value of ongoing liquidity.

It is also becoming more common for employers to take an interest in applicants' traces on the internet, increasing the pressure of presenting a flawless resume beyond the CV.

The business areas using personal data are widely scattered, they keep growing and only a selection of them can be outlined here. In each case, the goal lies in predicting the customer, whose needs and business risks can not only be identified but increasingly also predicted. As part of analytical customer relationship management, many service providers offer to analyse a customer's (buying) behaviour in order to draw new information from it and identify future patterns (predictive analytics). This can then be used to gain further insights into the customer lifecycle, derive new ways of addressing or identify susceptibility to competitor products. It has even become possible to predict the future liquidity of customers. Furthermore, personal analytics can assess customer value, give a termination forecast or provide information on typical investment behaviour.

The subject (as potential customer, business partner or employee) in all its complexity is replaced by a compilation of data whose commodifiable characteristics can now be selectively addressed by economic actors, which will be examined in more detail below.

4.3 The Personalised Interaction Between Physical Space and Cyberspace

As knowledge about customers increases, it is becoming easy for informed service providers to target them as data subjects. As described, given the diversity of data-based utilisation contexts, this address necessarily takes on different forms. It can take place in physical real space or in virtual space, but also as a mixed form in digitalised real space. It can take place through an immediate translation of collected data (sentient city) or it can refer to data compiled over a larger period in advance. Mixed forms are also common here, with direct customer targeting (e.g., personalised display advertising in a store) taking place based on collected data (for example, via the customer card). What the various ways of approaching customers with digitally stored knowledge share in common is that they convert individuals into potentially commodifiable characteristics in advance. It is not about capturing the complex personality of a target person, but primarily those characteristics that are relevant for a potential business. Instead of assessing the borrower's creditworthiness based on their personal appearance, the lender will direct his offers toward the exact items of available data sets. Online retailers primarily present products in line with the customer's identified preferences, with no interest in other personal attributes, and advertisers target their offers more closely to the user's specific preferences than to general trends.

For a deeper analysis, we will first look at the virtual translation of data into cyberspace offerings, where targeting based on user characteristics can take place immediately and in real time.

Addresses taking place via ad servers assign websites with different page content to different target groups in order to display the appropriate banner. What is appropriate is decided based on one or more characteristics sifted from the pool of all persons, or their IP address. Accordingly, the advertisement for a golf vacation for the target group of men over 50 will appear on a more sophisticated news site, while the ad for a soft drink for children is integrated into an online game. The time of the display or the regional reference can also be adjusted individually. More recently, semantic targeting, which addresses the user only in relevant editorial contexts, has been used for further individualisation. It has also become possible to evaluate developments within the pages, such as comments from readers (Aaltonen and Tempini 2014, p. 103ff).

While the focus here is on the recorded individual features or feature bundles and types that lead to a specified form of address, in other virtual spaces the derivation from the observed behaviour of many other users plays a central role for individualised targeting: If it can be demonstrated for many consumers that demand of X is followed by demand of Y, predictions can also be made for other users with corresponding behaviour patterns. This *collaborative filtering* allows conclusions to be drawn for sales items regarding the likelihood of a positive response. The "You might also be interested in this" notice is not only a central component of the business models of Amazon, Netflix or Google News, but is ubiquitous on the web.

Social networks like Facebook sort the wealth of user information they collect into databases that advertisers around the globe can access. Target groups can be defined by various criteria (e.g., location, age, gender, language, interests and behaviour) and addressed accordingly on their

Facebook page. For companies, tailored target groups can be sifted out using customer lists, website traffic or app activity. The ads can then be embedded in different ways (Desktop News Feed, Mobile News Feed, Right Column and Audience Network) and timed as desired. In this way, users are confronted at specific points in time on the desktop computer or mobile with messages that coincide with the range of topics relevant to them and with their specific preferences.

In all three cases, cyberspace is customised to the individual user, with the advertising company determining the relevant characteristics for addressing the respective customer. The advantages of cyberspace that seem to lie in its wider range of offers in comparison with the more segmented and restricted real space are partly lost as a result of the ubiquity of personalised, commercially exploitable content. Although this is by no means true for all content, this personalisation is present in various forms on most pages and is not always recognisable as such. This is particularly the case with native advertising, where messages are unobtrusively integrated into texts, videos, blogs and feeds. Depending on the channel, the layout of the message can be precisely adapted to the environment. The boundaries between the commercial and the public, the individually directed and the generally relevant are blurred by creating a feeling of familiarity and credibility (Schauster et al. 2016).

Turning from cyberspace to real space, the latter can also be personalised in the interplay with virtual data storages. The presentation of the various recording methods and the sketching of the networked city made it clear already that a strict separation of the two spheres was not sensible from the point of view of data generation. Such a dualism would ignore the numerous links between digital and analog sources, allowing for mutual enrichment precisely in their interplay. At the same time, it is often through the linking of the two spaces that the data collected actually become valuable. For example, with location-based services, the user's physical locations and routes are a valuable data add-on to the provider's database. The additional possibilities for collecting knowledge about customers even in sensitive areas or for predicting individual behaviour patterns can be related to this dataset (see also the examples of Cheung 2014; Michael and Michael 2011; Michael and Clarke 2013). Conversely, are taken out of virtual space and its processing capacities and put into value in real space. Many areas of marketing and personal services are becoming much more efficient with the influx of location-based data. Thanks to mobile phone data or wearables, the virtual user profile derived from clicks and entries is enhanced through real-space tracking, making it much more precise. Someone who frequently visits the local home improvement stores appears in the database as a potential loan borrower or reader of online articles related to home improvement. People who live in expensive neighbourhoods or frequently travel there on business might be interested in high-priced products.

The items about each individual, whether obtained virtually or derived from real space, create a corridor of personal life content and preferences, and addressing them within this corridor will lead to a successful transaction. From the supplier's perspective, preferences and opportunities have the highest chance of being directly converted into products and services when there is a correspondence between the two. When patterns of consumption are known, providers will direct their attention at those individuals who have the greatest potential interest in the product, message or service. Consequently, a highly filtered selection with a specific content reaches the respective target person, while unfamiliar things are withheld.

Here, beyond the generation of data, location-based services also serve to optimise the business environment. As locations and location-based activities are known and transmitted to data collectors in real time, on-site targeting can be realised based on the dispositions of the target person. Geofencing describes the automated triggering of an action in a predefined spatial section: The right products and services appear where the person is at a given moment, and they are offered in a way that appeals to them.

If real space can be restructured based on commercial criteria analogous to the further expansion of the internet, it will also end up offering a reproduction of the personality traits of an individual that are already known. Augmented reality applications have already taken such a step. They create hybrid, personalised worlds by presenting individually relevant content (Gong et al. 2017).

The further modern network technologies penetrate the everyday life of individuals; the more likely it becomes that the latter will be confronted with set pieces of and information about themselves. What is crucial is that this confrontation happens imperceptibly and that the time cannot be assessed. Furthermore, it tends to take place everywhere, as personalised data have long since left the virtual realm and can have an effect in both spheres. As is true for the workings of algorithms of large internet corporations, it is equally impossible to reconstruct why and based on what internet activities certain brochures end up in one's mailbox, why an ad appears on the smartphone at a certain point in the city, and to what extent an insurance policy taken out online is more or less expensive depending on the residential address.

4.4 Mirrored Spaces

"A world constructed from the familiar is a world in which there's nothing to learn. If personalization is too acute, it could prevent us from coming into contact with the mind-blowing, preconception-shattering experiences and ideas that change how we think about the world and ourselves". With this statement, Eli Pariser (2011, p. 9) outlined early on the constricting effect of personalised data utilisation that constantly provides internet users with a restricted and preselected range of information. Pariser popularised the term "filter bubble", which describes a personalised cyberspace that translates algorithmically collected data about each individual into information and offers that are as close and as intuitive to the user as possible. Based on identified preferences, people can be connected to information they are likely to be interested in, lured with incentives that have worked before and confronted with products that they will likely fancy. As these virtual offerings become more accessible than others, the result is a personalised stream of content offering users in the filter bubble fewer and fewer alternatives and choices. The filter bubble or echo chamber is like a *mirrored room* that emphasises the familiar and blocks out foreign elements. The mirror analogy expresses the self-referentiality of the viewer that is enforced in cyberspace via the externally controlled translation of the personally relevant. The environment becomes an image of one's own. Since only the one available version of the internet is being used, we do not notice what we are missing. In fact, however, in algorithmically curated information environments, the hit lists for search queries differ just as much as the content compilation on the entry page of the social network or the advertising offered next to an article.

Against this backdrop, Pariser and many others have repeatedly raised the question what such narrowed, fragmented world views mean for social cohesion and the political system when there are no collectively relevant topics left and the struggle for solutions in democratic discourse takes place without shared basic information (Bozdag and van den Hoven 2015; Spohr 2017). The public sphere is being replaced by closed communities whose members systematically isolate themselves from deviating realities, mutually reassuring each other within their filter bubbles. In this "balkanisation of cyberspace" then lies the danger of a multiple division of society, which in the long term will no longer be able to agree on what is relevant or to communicate at all about the same things. With respect to this challenge, the empirical findings on the filter bubble are mixed so far: While the study by Zuiderveen Borgesius et al. (2016) highlights the growing relevance of the debate about filter bubbles, it concludes that at this point there is no empirical evidence to justify a strong concern about filter bubbles (Ibid., p. 10). The large-scale study of around ten million U.S. Facebook users conducted by Bakshy et al. (2015) also indicates that it was not so much algorithmic ranking as personal choices that led to ideological demarcation. By contrast, other scholars have been able to identify ideological and partisan bubbles in Twitter discussions (Barberá et al. 2015; Boutyline and Willer 2017; Colleoni et al. 2014) and Facebook groups (Jacobson et al. 2016). Dylko et al. (2017) have demonstrated that the algorithmic preselection taking place on social network services like Facebook does favour the interaction with contents that confirm existing opinions and that the level of cognitive dissonance can be reduced effectively with algorithms operating in the background. Schmidt et al. (2017) also clearly confirm the thesis that news is consumed selectively. They analysed how often, how long and with whom 376 million Facebook users shared stories from 920 media outlets around the world between 2010 and 2015 and found out that most Facebook users only interact with a few news sources and prefer to share news from these portals with friends. The content and orientation of these portals are often the community that participates. In spite of the extreme diversity of offerings that exists in cyberspace, users move in self-selected clusters: "Despite the wide availability of content and heterogeneous narratives, there is major segregation and growing polarisation in online news consumption" (Schmidt et al. 2017, p. 3038).

Psychologically, bubbles can be explained as the result of our avoidance of cognitive dissonance, i.e., the desire of humans to reconcile their different cognitions, such as perceptions, thoughts or attitudes, without contradictions. But it is only cyberspace and its algorithmically tailored offerings that allow people to banish other realities in a consistent and systematic way. Defining oneself via the clicks made leads into a virtual environment which in turn encourages *recursive use*. The tendency to selectively choose news that reflects one's own opinion and attitude ("selective exposure") takes on a double direction in the internet age: It is not just the user picking out the information, but the information is also precisely tailored to each individual user. As outlined above, this has become possible and commonplace on the basis of comprehensive tracking and targeting.

While it is becoming increasingly obvious that information bubbles are having an impact in cyberspace, and issues associated with it (such as fake news, election manipulation, and the loss of social cohesion) are the topic of numerous feature articles, confirming Eli Pariser, little has been said on the socio-economic implications of the filter bubble. For an evaluation of the new options for action in cyberspace, however, its inherent self-referentiality is extremely relevant: The spaces provided by the private sector convert the user into personalised offers and information. The structures in cyberspace, ostensibly free of charge, are paid for click by click with the user's own transparency, bringing that which can be commercialised ever closer to the individual. In the mirrored spaces of cyberspace, users primarily see themselves. Increasingly, everybody is confronted with offers, information and contacts that resemble their known preferences.

There are various reasons why the known and familiar reach the user more easily and are embedded as a fixed rule of assignment in the algorithmically organised space: In connection with the digital habitus, it has already been emphasised how difficult it is to appropriate digital content outside one's own milieu. Entering environments on the internet that are unfamiliar and hard to predict requires more effort than staying in one's personal comfort zone. As outlined, however, putting too much emphasis on the tendency to stick to the familiar would mean ignoring the opportunities for capital acquisition. Access to resources in cyberspace is, in principle, open—for those who are willing, motivated and receive guidance, for example, from an educational institution. With increasing transparency of the customer, however, this access is obscured in that cyberspace, as a sequence of virtual spaces, does not keep its rigid structure, but constantly offers itself to the user anew in a changed form. Because of cyberspace's ability to turn the socially familiar into its content, it becomes more likely that users will persist in this space. In the mirrored room, everyone is surrounded by the known and familiar.

Numerous studies demonstrate a higher effectiveness of those messages that are aligned with the personality traits of the target person (for an overview, see Hirsh et al. 2012). Since these messages in cyberspace are aligned to the user's activities, the requested pages can be equipped with specific stimuli, which in turn make the next step in virtual space more likely. Priming via image, sound or speech leads to the activation of implicit memory content, which specifically influences feelings and subsequent behaviour. In the same way, the offerings of cyberspace can be enhanced with framing effects, where variations of the same message can be used to influence the user's behaviour in different ways. In this way, the virtual context that reflects the user's specific interests can be selectively furnished with reinforcing content (Wu and Cheng 2011).

Users´ tendency to view content that is familiar can also be explained psychologically by the mere exposure effect, which means that people will develop a preference for something as a result of repeated exposure. This effect can be used to explain the demand for certain content by the conditioning of the user, whose choices are influenced by past experiences. Messages can then be formulated accordingly. For instance, repeating an advertisement can help ensure that the consumer will perceive it positively. The more an individual likes a specific stimulus and the more they associate it with pleasant feelings, the better this works (Felser 2015, p. 81ff).

In terms of opportunities for social advancement, the personalised structure of cyberspace implies significant limitations. The opportunity to acquire cultural and social capital has been related to overcoming site effects and being able to participate. In a hierarchically constituted real space, there are obstacles such as physical inaccessibility and distance, the lack of visibility and the social distance to the target group, which cyberspace seems to eliminate in part. But on closer inspection, the available offerings of the digitally mediated supply structure are now transformed into personalised offerings that reflexively use that which exists already: Accessing a song on Spotify or a video on YouTube will result in suggestions that are very similar to what has been requested before. Ordering clothes on Amazon will lead to new offers of the same style. Once interest in a product has been expressed, it is used to shape the virtual environment in different forms, and the display's automatic word recognition system automatically reformulates past entries. The opportunity to obtain resources relevant for upward mobility is therefore impeded structurally. In the seemingly hierarchy-free environment of cyberspace, what has to be overcome is no longer just the filter of relevance inherent in the habitus. Rather, it is the ability of broad areas of cyberspace to exactly adapt to this habitus, to mirror it, displacing alternative as well as instructive contexts of experience and education. In the process of digital socialisation, serendipity, the accidental discovery of something not sought after, something enriching, becomes less likely. Whether information on cultural and leisure events, political discourse, relevant news or the latest consumer trends: All of them are ordered in cyberspace according to the preferences stored in data sets. They refer to and revisit the contextual and compositional factors in the socialisation process.

This recursivity characterises the acquisition of social capital as well: Right after logging on to Facebook for the first time, the user is assigned to numerous people they have met in the past at school, at their place of residence or at their job training. In the mirrored space of cyberspace, the opportunity to cultivate social capital emphasised in Chapter 3.2 (Ellison et al. 2011; Steinfield et al. 2008, among others) is impeded by an algorithmically driven selection that largely refers to the same social context that already shaped the user in the past. The fields of interest to be assigned to each individual and the locations communicated algorithmically in the network, which could serve to initiate further contacts, also frequently reflect user properties. Without the need to log in, the IP address already reveals the current location of the user and provides specific information. The map service settings are location-based, selected shopping suggestions and events refer in particular to the known real space, and travel recommendations are in line with interests expressed in the past. For the segments of the population lacking in capital, their personalised cyberspace will not contain ads for the theatre, or the public square mentioned earlier or references to exclusive vacation spots for the rich, despite the fact that there are no actual physical distances or social distinction processes at work. Virtual spaces of opportunity simply become less visible for the individual. Unfortunately, the isolated use of cyberspace always ensures that actions in the virtual cannot be perceived in alignment with the outside world. The danger is that cyberspace is then perceived not as a variant of reality, but as absolute reality.

However, the decreasing probability of being able to perceive resources that are foreign to one's milieu or habitus in mirrored spaces is only one—albeit quite central—consequence of the economic exploitation of personal data. Connecting some of the business areas outlined above with the individual's options for action reveals further limitations: Depending on the utilisation context and the corresponding coding of the framework of action, the externally controlled regimentation must present itself differently based on collected data. While online ads or suggested news content merely provide an effective incentive that the user can decide to skip, the data-based assignment of a specific risk score means that "unsuitable" offers—for example, in online insurance, loans or health insurance premiums—are systematically withheld from the customer and "suitable" offers are suggested instead. The decision on what is appropriate for the user and what will reach them is based on the relevance of the available data as defined by the respective business field. Such forms of "social sorting" were compiled early on by David Lyon in his Surveillance Studies (Lyon 2003). Lyon focuses on the public and private-sector forms of group and personal data processing, describing the enabling or disabling of actions depending on the selection characteristic (gender, ethnicity, occupation, social status, etc.). Again, the code functions here as an "invisible door" that determines who has access to experiences, events and information and which parts of the population can interact and participate (Ibid., p. 13, p. 23ff). The opportunity to explore cyberspace independent of the available capital is clearly revealed as an illusion. All markers of inequality such as income, education or social status can be systematically used to constitute cyberspace, resulting in spaces that differ in how they are equipped and in how they can be accessed. The above-mentioned inaccessibility in real space due to barriers or distances corresponds to a virtual space that regulates access to resources on a user-specific basis. In addition, contents of cyberspace can also be completely faded out, eliminating the ability to perceive other options.

Finally, algorithmic decision procedures also influence the third obstacle to capital acquisition described above, which is social distance. To begin with, it was stressed how segments of the population lacking in capital could strategically conceal the habitus, temporarily relieving themselves from having to know and apply the rules of distinction. However, as has been outlined, a consistent valorisation of personal data takes effect at an earlier stage, as the virtual environment is already pre-structured by the registered dispositions of the user. The habitus is already known and virtual content refers to its different aspects to varying degrees. The opportunity to take advantage of resources that facilitate social advancement is predefined in an unequal manner.

Moreover, it is evident that the available information about a person moves back and forth between cyberspace and physical real space, and in both spaces this information can be used either to create an incentive or to impose rules. Things like individual reliability scores, a person's health or special consumer preferences not only result in a personalised address in cyberspace, but also have a direct influence on the everyday life of each individual in real space and their options for action and perception.

4.5 Interim Conclusion: Digital Self-Confrontation

The use of cyberspace, the internet and other networked objects is accompanied by the accumulation of personalised data. While the internet is praised as a medium that can transform the boundaries of individual experience, turning spatial mobility into social mobility, making actual use of this potential requires the individual to engage in constant self-measuring. New products and technologies such as the Internet of Things, cloud services, sensors and countless smartphone applications represent the foundations of such measuring. While it can be countered with knowledge and technical effort, avoiding it completely is almost impossible.

While the permanent provision of data within these structural specifications has been analysed from the perspective of surveillance, interpreting the consequences of a "culture of self-exposure" as a voluntary disciplinary process (Bauman and Lyon 2013; Lyon 2018; Michael and Michael 2010; Zuboff 2019, among others), the recursive aspects of a digitally influenced socialisation call for a different focus: There are strong indications that the self-referential use of digital technologies is closely related to the social question. Across all basic functions of existence, many new options for action can be identified in cyberspace and in networked real space, all primarily addressing the familiar. What clearly stands out in such a mirrored space is that customers are increasingly addressed with products and services which they are known to like and be familiar with and which fit into their living environment and budget. It is equally obvious that each individual is left in the place where they are with their specific habitus.

Cyberspace, which could initially be described as an arrangement that can be accessed easily and experienced anonymously, hardly has any isolated niches left that can be explored without being tracked. Based on the evaluation of personal data, users enter each area with specific indexes that assess them and that can be exchanged within the virtual sphere. Such an exchange, which is able to personalise spaces in advance, leaves users with limited options, which means that the resources available in cyberspace are also structured by accessibility and perception.

What each individual obtains from cyberspace or through interconnected devices ultimately impacts everyday experiences in the real world, whether it be internet acquaintances, vacation recommendations, shopping addresses or leisure tips. In addition, transmitter–receiver systems are active in smart real space, which can selectively display, hide or regulate, again resulting in a recursive acquisition, as has been illustrated by numerous examples. The field of social contacts, preferred places or shops then provide an opportunity structure with numerous feedback or place effects all standing in the way of cross-milieu acquisition. Beyond the filtered use of services in cyberspace (contacts, advertising, financing offers), it is also filtered offerings that have an impact on the options for action and perception in real space—and which inevitably influence the possibilities for the constitution of space. The process of "mirroring" takes place across spaces.

Up to this point, the demonstrated relativisation of opportunities of capital acquisition can serve as a new starting point to reflect on digital offerings in relation to education. Beyond the inequalities of digital access and use, the main point is that the opportunity to obtain resources digitally can be predefined by all the user's characteristics. It is therefore not only about having the skills to use a computer for education and resource acquisition, but also about knowing under which conditions these resources can reach a user at all.

For the study's overarching objective, which is the examination of current stratification processes in the context of digitalisation, the focus on cyberspace and the processes in real space influenced by it is not yet sufficient. So far, cyberspace has been conceptualised as a strategic option of choice, and this includes the possibility of consistently choosing to turn away from the effects of datasets. According to this assumption, the many links created by the use of smartphones or certain gadgets can be severed by digital abstinence. This would leave mainly automated capture systems such as cameras, RFID technologies or intelligent networked devices and their increasing prevalence as mediators of possibilities or restrictions.

As a matter of fact, the data-driven economy is encroaching on everyday life regardless of an individual's affinity for computer use, ownership of a smartphone or the presence of sender-receiver systems. As shown by the multiple forms of data acquisition and exchange, personal information from numerous channels flows together without immediately being commodified in a specific context. Extensive personal data about each individual are stockpiled in databases that are generally invisible and sold by global traders. Regardless of the context in which they are collected, these data facilitate personalised offerings for a wide variety of utilisation contexts. Information on individuals has thus become completely disconnected from the data collection infrastructure, and for a fee it can be monetised offline at any time.

This billion-dollar data trading market should also be highly relevant in the context of the opportunity of capital acquisition. If virtual offerings can potentially define individual scopes of possibility, then this needs to be considered also for traded, decontextualised data. How does their use affect the question of situational (dis-)advantage in the urban space with its unequal opportunities? To find an answer, we must take a further step and transfer the data merchants' products back to individual cities.

REFERENCES

Aaltonen, Aleksi & Tempini, Niccoló (2014): Everything Counts in Large Amounts: A Critical Realist Case Study on Data-based Production. *Journal of Information Technology* 29 (1), 97–110.

Amoore, Louise & Piotukh, Volha (eds.) (2016): *Algorithmic Life: Calculative Devices in the Age of Big Data*. London, New York: Routledge.

Bakshy, Eytan; Messing, Solomon & Adamic, Lada A. (2015): Political Science. Exposure to Ideologically Diverse News and Opinion on Facebook. *Science* 348 (6239), 1130–1132.

Barberá, Pablo; Jost, John T.; Nagler, Jonathan; Tucker, Joshua A. & Bonneau, Richard (2015): Tweeting From Left to Right: Is Online Political Communication More Than an Echo Chamber? *Psychological Science* 26 (10), 1531–1542.

Bauman, Zygmunt & Lyon, David (2013): *Daten, Drohnen, Disziplin. Ein Gespräch über flüchtige Überwachung*. Berlin: Suhrkamp.

Blattberg, Robert C.; Kim, Byung-Do & Neslin, Scott A. (2008): *Database marketing. Analyzing and managing customers*. New York: Springer.

Boutyline, Andrei & Willer, Robb (2017): The Social Structure of Political Echo Chambers: Variation in Ideological Homophily in Online Networks. *Political Psychology* 38 (3), 551–569.

Bozdag, Engin & van den Hoven, Jeroen (2015): Breaking the Filter Bubble: Democracy and Design. *Ethics and Information Technology* 17 (4), 249–265.

Bujlow, Tomasz; Carela-Español, Valentín; Solé-Pareta, Josep; & Barlet-Ros Pere (2017): A Survey on Web Tracking: Mechanisms, Implications, and Defenses. *Proceedings of the IEEE* 105 (8), 1476–1510.

Cheung, Anne S.Y. (2014): Location Privacy: The Challenges of Mobile Service Devices. *Computer Law & Security Review* 30 (1), 41–54.

Cocchia, Annalisa (2014): Smart and Digital City: A Systematic Literature Review. In: Renata Paola Dameri & Camille Rosenthal-Sabroux (eds.): *Smart City. How to Create Public and Economic Value with High Technology in Urban Space*. Cham: Springer, 13–43.

Colleoni, Elanor; Rozza, Alessandro & Arvidsson, Adam (2014): Echo Chamber or Public Sphere? Predicting Political Orientation and Measuring Political Homophily in Twitter Using Big Data. *Journal of Communication* 64 (2), 317–332.

Crang, Michel & Graham, Stephen (2007): Sentient Cities: Ambient Intelligence and the Politics of Urban Space. *Information, Communication & Society* 10 (6), 789–817.

Cuijpers, Colette & Koops, Bert-Jaap (2013): Smart Metering and Privacy in Europe: Lessons from the Dutch Case. In: Serge Gutwirth, Ronald Leenes, Paul de Hert & Yves Poullet (eds.): *European Data Protection: Coming of Age*. Dordrecht: Springer Netherlands, 269–293.

Dameri, Renata Paola & Rosenthal-Sabroux, Camille (eds.) (2014): *Smart City. How to Create Public and Economic Value with High Technology in Urban Space*. Cham: Springer.

Droste, Friedrich (2014): *Die strategische Manipulation der elektronischen Mundpropaganda. Eine spieltheoretische Analyse*. Wiesbaden: Springer Gabler.

Dwyer, Catherine (2009): Behavioral Targeting: A Case Study of Consumer Tracking on Levis.com. *Proceedings of the Fifteenth Americas Conference on Information Systems*, 1–10.

Dylko, Ivan; Dolgov, Igor; Hoffman, William; Eckhart, Nicholas; Molina, Maria & Aaziz, Omar (2017): The Dark Side of Technology: An Experimental Investigation of the Influence of Customizability Technology on Online Political Selective Exposure. *Computers in Human Behavior* 73, 181–190.

Ellison, Nicole B.; Steinfield, Charles & Lampe, Cliff (2011): Connection Strategies: Social Capital Implications of Facebook-enabled Communication Practices. *New Media & Society* 13 (6), 873–892.

Eubanks, Virginia (2018): *Automating Inequality. How High-Tech Tools Profile, Police and Punish the Poor*. New York: St Martin's Press.

Felser, Georg (2015): *Werbe- und Konsumentenpsychologie*. Berlin, Heidelberg: Springer-Verlag Berlin Heidelberg.

Gong, Huiwen; Hassink, Robert & Maus, Gunnar (2017): What does Pokémon Go teach us about geography? *Geographica Helvetica* 72 (2), 227–230.

Greenspan, Anna (2021): QR Codes and the Sentient City. *Studia Neophilologica* 93 (2), 206–218.

Herland, Matthew; Khoshgoftaar, Taghi M. & Wald, Randall (2014): A review of data mining using big data in health informatics. *Journal of Big Data* 1 (2), 1-35.

Hilbert, Martin & López, Priscila (2011): The World's Technological Capacity to Store, Communicate, and Compute Information. *Science* 332 (6025), 60–65.
Hirsh, Jacob B.; Kang, Sonia K. & Bodenhausen, Galen V. (2012): Personalized Persuasion: Tailoring Persuasive Appeals to Recipients' Personality Traits. *Psychological Science* 23 (6), 578–581.
Hotho, Andreas; Pedersen, Rasmus Ulslev & Wurst, Michael (2010): Ubiquitous Data. In: Michael May & Lorenza Saitta (eds.): *Ubiquitous Knowledge Discovery*. Berlin, Heidelberg: Springer, 61–74.
Jacobson, Susan; Myung, Eunyoung & Johnson, Steven L. (2016): Open Media or Echo Chamber: The Use of Links in Audience Discussions on the Facebook Pages of Partisan News Organizations. *Information, Communication & Society* 19 (7), 875–891.
Jin, Haojian; Yang, Zhijian; Kumar, Swarun & Hong, Jason (2018): Towards Wearable Everyday Body-Frame Tracking using Passive RFIDs. *Proceedings of ACM on Interactive, Mobile, Wearable and Ubiquitous Technologies* 1 (4), 1–23.
Khoury, Muin J. & Ioannidis, John (2014): Medicine. Big Data Meets Public Health. *Science* 346 (6213), 1054–1055.
Kitchin, Rob & Dodge, Martin (2011): *Code/Space: Software and Everyday Life*. Cambridge: MIT Press.
Kreutzer, Ralf & Land, Karl-Heinz (2015): *Digital Darwinism. Branding and Business Models in Jeopardy*. Berlin, Heidelberg: Springer.
Lyon, David (2018): *The Culture of Surveillance*. Cambridge: Polity.
Lyon, David (Hrsg.) (2003): *Surveillance as Social Sorting: Privacy, Risk, and Digital Discrimination*. London, New York: Routledge.
Michael, Katina & Clarke, Roger (2013): Location and Tracking of Mobile Devices: Überveillance Stalks the Streets. *Computer Law & Security Review* 29 (3), 216–228.
Michael, Katina & Michael, M. G. (2011): The Social and Behavioural Implications Of Location-based Services. *Journal of Location Based Services* 5 (3-4), 121–137.
Millonig, Alexandra & Gartner, Georg (2011): Identifying Motion and Interest Patterns of Shoppers for Developing Personalized Wayfinding Tools. *Journal of Location Based Services* 3 (1), 3–21.
O' Mahony, Stephen (2015): A Proposed Model for the Approach to Augmented Reality Deployment in Marketing Communications. *Procedia—Social and Behavioral Sciences* (175), 227–235. Online: https://isiarticles.com/bundles/Article/pre/pdf/41113.pdf (01.03.2023)
Pariser, Eli (2011): *Filter Bubble. What the Internet is Hiding from you*. New York: The Penguin Press.
Power, Daniel, J. (2015): Creating a Data-Driven Global Society. In: Iyer Lakshmi & Daniel, J. Power (eds.): *Reshaping Society through Analytics,*

Collaboration, and Decision Support. Role of Business Intelligence and Social Media. Cham: Springer, 13–28.

Safransky, Sara (2020): Geographies of Algorithmic Violence: Redlining the Smart City. *International Journal of Urban and Regional Research* 44 (2), 200–218.

Schauster, Erin. E.; Ferrucci, Patrick & Neill, Marlene S. (2016): Native Advertising Is the New Journalism: How Deception Affects Social Responsibility. *American Behavioral Scientist* (6), 1–17.

Schmidt, Ana Lucía; Zollo, Fabiana; Del Vicario, Michela; Bessi, Alessandro; Scala, Antonio; Caldarelli, Guido et al. (2017): Anatomy of news consumption on Facebook. *Proceedings of the National Academy of Sciences of the United States of America* 114 (12), 3035-3039.

Shepard, Marc (ed.) (2011): *Sentient City. Ubiquitous Computing, Architecture, and the Future of Urban Space*. Cambridge: MIT Press.

Spohr, Dominic (2017): Fake News and Ideological Polarization: Filter Bubbles and Selective Exposure on Social Media. *Business Information Review* 34 (3), 150–160.

Steinfield, Charles; Ellison, Nicole B. & Lampe, Cliff (2008): Social Capital, Self-esteem, and Use of Online Social Network Sites: A Longitudinal Analysis. *Journal of Applied Developmental Psychology* 29 (6), 434–445.

Thrift, Nigel (2014): The 'Sentient' City and What It May Portend. *Big Data & Society* 1 (1), 1–21.

Wu, Chin-Shan & Cheng, Fei-Fei (2011): The Joint Effect of Framing and Anchoring on Internet Buyers' Decision-making. *Electronic Commerce Research and Applications* 10 (3), 358–368.

Yadav, Mayank; Joshi, Yatish & Rahman, Zillur (2015): Mobile Social Media: The New Hybrid Element of Digital Marketing Communications. *Procedia—Social and Behavioral Sciences* 189, 335–343.

Zuboff, Shoshana (2019): *The Age of Surveillance Capitalism: The Fight for a Human Future at the New Frontier of Power*. London: Profile Books

Zuiderveen Borgesius, Frederik J.; Trilling, Damian; Möller, Judith; Bodó, Balázs; Vreese, Claes H. de & Helberger, Natali (2016): Should We Worry About Filter Bubbles? *Internet Policy Review* 5 (1), 1–11.

Open Access This chapter is licensed under the terms of the Creative Commons Attribution 4.0 International License (http://creativecommons.org/licenses/by/4.0/), which permits use, sharing, adaptation, distribution and reproduction in any medium or format, as long as you give appropriate credit to the original author(s) and the source, provide a link to the Creative Commons license and indicate if changes were made.

The images or other third party material in this chapter are included in the chapter's Creative Commons license, unless indicated otherwise in a credit line to the material. If material is not included in the chapter's Creative Commons license and your intended use is not permitted by statutory regulation or exceeds the permitted use, you will need to obtain permission directly from the copyright holder.

CHAPTER 5

Decontextualised Data and Socio-Spatial Differences

Abstract This chapter presents (personalised) data as commodities and demonstrates the related contexts of utilisation. Making concrete the possibilities of recursive reference in the data economy, we return to the physical environment: Using commercially traded data for the cities of Berlin, Munich and Essen, an exemplary and empirical study examines in what manner a data-based logic of utilisation reaches the different districts and their inhabitants and the implications this carries for socialisation and the overall social question.

Keywords Data traders · Personalised marketing · Opportunity structure · Site effects

One reason why it is so difficult to grasp the far-reaching significance of personal data lies in their immateriality. The zeros and ones, to name only the most basic form of their visualisation, convey a harmless abstraction that stands in stark contrast to the influence the translations of this code can have in the real world. What makes the process of data collection and addressing more tangible is the physical visibility of the devices that accomplish this and by the immediate compensation that they offer. A digital voice assistant that can convert commands into information and services, a Skype call that makes the conversation partner immediately visible, or the use of a digital address book are examples of how with the help of technology, data are expressed in useful services.

In the types of recursive acquisition described so far, the relationship between entry and use was still partly visible as both happened through the same medium. In cyberspace, personalised advertising, news or search results sorted by their relevance appear in the same virtual environment into which a large part of the processed data flowed before. Similarly, location-based services, access control via RFID chips or advertising insertion through facial recognition in networked real space are often still recognisable as interacting systems.

By contrast, the possibility of isolating personal data from the technical context of their collection removes any attributability that would imply at least some form of control. As an immaterial commodity, individual attributions "go on a journey" and are then again presented to the user in the form of a service. In the meantime, they are subject to analyses, additions, copies and recombinations undertaken by decentralised management systems, crossing borders and legal jurisdictions. Their fluidity is not immediately apparent in real life. Generally, users do not know what they have lost, nor to whom. The various sources remain as abstract as the different utilisation contexts. Most people notice this surveillance only in the form of personalised advertising and do not consider this cause for great concern. In fact, the utilisation contexts of personal data produce a tight grid that predetermines opportunities for participation and access to resources.

The goal is therefore to concretise the diagnosed mechanisms of recursivity for traded data and to examine the social and space-constituting consequences of their capitalisation. Two sets of questions are of interest here: How does the data-based addressing of the target person or group take place and which attributes come into play in the context of Bourdieu's field of social positions? And second, what structural influence do the traded data have on space and neighbourhood?

To answer both questions, it was necessary to gain empirical access to the data market. Its offer structure becomes apparent via the portfolios of data traders on the internet. A more in-depth analysis of the available customer data is achieved, by way of example, by extracting an extensive data set comprising the households of major German cities.

5.1 Data as an Unequally Used Commodity

Over the years, the collection, processing and utilisation of data has grown into a market worth billions of euros, with well over 1,000 participating companies in Germany alone (Goldhammer and Wiegand 2017, p. 21). In addition to companies that collect customer data online and offline, a large number of data brokers specialise in the processing of personal data of specific target groups for the credit industry, advertising, insurance, consulting or job placement, among others. The data can be sold directly to interested parties; they can be viewed for a fee or sold as an analysis result abstracted from the data set. In each case, it is once again the increasing transparency of the customer which is rediscovered as a prerequisite for economic success in the age of digitalisation.

The power to create this transparency is thus not necessarily limited to the immediate environment of the data-generating technologies or those who commission a personal address for commercial reasons. For the data trade, the centre of this power is where data acquisition and utilisation are coordinated. With many providers, especially large platforms such as Facebook or Google, the collection of data and their downstream trading lie in one hand.

As the data can be substituted, data traders can derive missing attributes from an existing data set or compensate for them with higher-level target group references. As a consequence, data subjects are addressed with data that were not collected directly through them, allowing for the data stock to be further enhanced and supplemented by characteristics that are essential for a personalised categorisation. At the same time, individual addresses can be substituted by the behaviour of other individuals as long as they belong to the same target group. Above, the term collaborative filtering was used to describe one form of this collective address ("Customers who bought this also like that"). Because of these substitution practices, even people who are very careful about the data they share are addressed more or less directly. Most importantly, the mutual exchange and purchase of data provides data traders with comprehensive portfolios. While they achieve size and the associated economies of scale through exchange, what this cross-border trade means for the data subject is a diffusion of data and total loss of transparency. The specific utilisation of the available data can then have an impact in all areas of life. Individuals are confronted with "ubiquitous data" coming from many different, loosely coupled, and sometimes overlapping sources in an asynchronous and decentralised way (Hotho et al. 2010, p. 62), addressing them individually or collectively, making it impossible for them to gain control over these data. The described interplay of online and offline now has to be understood inter-temporally and across spaces: Anything that has been stored about an individual can be used to address them anywhere, with no transparency whatsoever.

Consequently, there is a strong asymmetry of information between the data subject and the recipient or distributor of personal data. Based on the revenue generated, the trader can accurately estimate the value of the data. For consumers, on the other hand, it is almost impossible to understand in what form and context their data are being traded. To determine the value of their data, consumers would need to know, among other things, at what points and under what conditions the data are monetised, how long they are stored and economically usable, they would need to take into account risks of misuse and their consequences and they would need to be able to assess all indirect derivations from the existing data sets (cf. Wiewiorra 2018, p. 464f). Furthermore, economically harmful effects on different areas of consumers' lives because of market entry barriers or price discrimination (e.g., loans, insurance) would have to be considered.

Since consumers do not have this information and do not share in the profits generated with their data, economic value creation is distributed very unevenly. Although there is a general idea of the value of individual data in parts of society, so far there are very few paths toward an alternative valorisation of personal data that would bypass the databases of platform operators and traders. Some health insurance providers and insurance companies do offer discounts for data, but they fail to reveal to their clients how much they actually gain.

Most consumers agree to receive nothing more than the access to digital services in exchange for their data—a fact that can be explained with the double novelty of these goods of exchange. While individual data capital as a new currency is something that needs to be discovered and assessed by everyone individually, the data economy also offers specialised services. These are commonplace by now, but at the same time still seem fascinating; to some, they are considered indispensable, and in general they are perceived as an important novelty, their actual value hard to determine. In this perspective, the special opportunity for digital participation more than outweighs the abstract way in which information is disclosed (Acquisti et al. 2013).

In the current system of the data economy, an objective economic profit can only be achieved if the disclosure of data is accompanied by an economic benefit that exceeds the costs incurred. In this context, the opportunities for acquiring capital by gaining social and cultural capital in cyberspace have been examined. The preliminary conclusion is sobering: Even in digitalised real space, profits in the data trade are based on a monetisation of knowledge which is then used by businesses to create individualised offers. While on the supply side data capital can thus be converted into economic capital, on the demand side it grants access to use that can be converted into material profit only to a limited extent. Access mainly leads into mirrored spaces, and this makes a transformation into economic capital more difficult for the segments of the population lacking capital. In other words: Data capital can be monetised very well under recursive effects, which means that the data traders benefit, and users lose out. If, because of the characteristics that haven been described, data are collected without any compensation for the data subject, all the profit generated by the digital business goes only to one side.

The databases (portfolios) of the data traders should reveal this unequal utilisation of digital capital. With the permanent establishment of a data-aggregating system, these portfolios should reflect the returns of many years. At the same time, the associated possibilities of a personalised address reveal the extent to which data trading is the cause for the recursive logic.

5.2 Data Traders and Their Portfolio

In their range of services, data and address traders have different focal points. Their overriding interest lies in comprehensive information about each customer, which allows targeted addressing, increases the probability of conversion, protects companies against default risks, enables cost reductions and impact measurements and, last but not least, allows for the planning of processes and behavioural predictions (Pentland et al. 2021 for an overview). What all these offerings share in common is an extensive data set that, depending on the business partner's specific needs, makes a customised selection possible.

Large providers on the international market (such as Acxiom, Experian, or CoreLogic) maintain customer profiles, company addresses and e-mail contacts amounting to several million each. Numerous additional features on consumer behaviour, socio-demographics or housing and living situation are systematically processed. They offer precise query options ranging from "likelihood of switching health insurance" to "affinity for bargain shopping" and "travel type" and provide detailed information on sales-relevant categories such as education, income, health, lifestyle and class. Information that can be retrieved immediately includes household income, credit score, social class and corresponding interests. In addition, data on different product fields can be obtained, and in many cases preferences are already pre-sorted.

A look at the extensive portfolios of data traders on the internet also reveals the possibilities for addressing customers (e.g., www.az-direct.com): Options include postal or e-mail address, display marketing campaigns such as banner advertising as well as ads in search engines and social networks. In addition, they offer forms of mobile marketing, where a commercial message appears based on location or weather, for example, via the apps installed on a smart phone. Numerous possibilities of linking online and offline appear here: As part of a CRM onboarding, for example, the intersection between existing customers from the company's own database and the users of various internet platforms can be identified in order to reach them with a targeted digital campaign. This can be supplemented by an offline campaign, such as catalog mailings. The networked real space in turn lends itself to digital out-of-home campaigns, where digital outdoor displays are already linked to various targeting criteria such as local reference, weather or time of day, and segments can be programmatically controlled via addressable TV (cf. www.acxiom.de/).

As expected, all these providers stress the conformity of their services with current data protection regulations. Aside from refraining from the collection of specific types of personal data (such as race or ethnicity, political or religious views, information about gender or sexual orientation) as required by law, data traders refer to consents given or to the legitimate interests of them and their partners and clients. In Europe, regulations are comparatively strict; however, the abundance of data available makes it hard to believe that laws can limit the volume of data significantly. In countries with fewer regulations on data protection, data vendors' offers surpass the European market:

As early as 2014, the federal consumer protection agency of the United States, the Federal Trade Commission, conducted an in-depth investigation of nine of the country's largest data trading companies. The results revealed a nearly complete coverage of all U.S. households with diverse labels. The Commission's summary of the enormous volume, most of which was generated without consumers' knowledge, includes the following statements: "Of the nine data brokers, one data broker's database has information on 1.4 billion consumer transactions and over 700 billion aggregated data elements; another data broker's database covers one trillion dollars in consumer transactions; and yet another data broker adds three billion new records each month to its databases. Most importantly, data brokers hold a vast array of information on individual consumers. For example, one of the nine data brokers has 3000 data segments for nearly every U.S. consumer" (Federal Trade Commission 2014, IV). The report also revealed an intensive exchange of data between individual traders, which greatly expands the data sets to the benefit of all parties involved. As in the German market, specific groups are derived from all the data obtained, ranging from individual characteristics such as "High-End Shopper", "Diabetest Interest" or "Home Ownership Status" to specific categorisations such as "Rural Everlasting" (single men or women aged 66 and older with a low educational level and small assets) (cf. Ibid., pp. 24f and V). Such groups can be used for the creation and sale of valuable lists for various usage contexts. A constant update of preferences, activities, memberships or address data is guaranteed at all times.

A closer look at the target groups reveals quite different customer groups. One of the references of AZ Direct in Germany, for example, is a fashion manufacturer for tall women whose market entry was facilitated by data analysis. Other customers include a foreign direct bank which advertises loans tailored to the individual financial situation or a TV station which was able to further differentiate its advertising for the male target group. Acxiom Germany lists an automobile manufacturer as one of its references that was able to improve the marketing of its SUVs by matching the customer list with the users of a social media platform as well as another online platform, and a cruise company that acquired new customers via a target group selection by using online and offline channels. These examples make it clear that the stored data assets reach individuals in virtual space as well as in real space in different contexts, targeting them individually or as part of a customer segment.

One important form of customer segmentation that is offered by almost all data traders is via geographical criteria. In addition to macro-geographic divisions (states, cities, or municipalities), data traders often have microgeographic segments, which are spaces of living and everyday life shared by people with the same values or lifestyle or from similar milieus. Campaigns can then be targeted to location-based features. The available data allow for a space-based target market selection and also provide street and building directories for whole areas. Individual characteristics can be assigned to these, so that spatial clusters with specific characteristics can be addressed collectively or individual units can be addressed individually.

Overall, the offers clearly reveal the possibilities offered by data trading companies for targeting consumers. This applies to the scope of the data, their precision and the available analysis capacities, as well as the many professionally mastered channels of an address.

With the trading of geo data and forms of address in real space, the residential environment again becomes a focus of attention. The negative effects of disadvantaged neighbourhoods on their residents in terms of socialisation and the ability to constitute space were discussed above. In this context, access to cyberspace was considered as a form of individual empowerment within an alternative opportunity structure, which then revealed its limited potential because of a new form of recursivity. As data traders refer to residential areas, are consumers again defined in ways that hinder their advancement?

So far, the commercial translations of individual characteristics have been described as recursive effects, which—as shown clearly by the offers of the data traders—individuals are confronted with in quite different ways. The place of residence is relevant here as the address that makes it possible to contact the (potential) customer with offers in real space. Beyond that, however, address and neighbourhood also provide information about dispositions and preferences of their residents, allowing for—as underscored by the data traders' advertising—more far-reaching deductions. For example, geo-scoring can be used to attribute specific needs or assess someone's creditworthiness. However, via the additional possibility of tracing action spaces, the acquisition of geo data also influences the constitution of space. The deliberate placement of advertising is one example, but it goes even further.

Taking a closer look at how customers are addressed in particular, but also at the significance of a person's address and neighbourhood in the context of data trading, the following section will directly apply purchasable geo data to individual neighbourhoods in German cities. The nature of the data and the traders' associated offers point to utilisation contexts that have different social effects in each neighbourhood.

5.3 Empirical Findings in the Socially Segmented Urban Space

For a more detailed definition of the empirical focus, we will return to the starting point: Above, we looked at the interdependence between available capital and residential area. While the residential location and situation depend on economic resources, these resources also help finance the conditions which enable or limit residents: Physical, social as well as image-related circumstances go along with certain socialisation influences (contextual and compositional factors), and they determine to what degree further capital can be obtained. There exists a fundamental social inequality of opportunity which unfolds fully only in a spatial perspective.

The fewer resources a spatial opportunity structure offers, the greater the disadvantage of its inhabitants in relation to neighbourhoods rich in capital. But how polarised are cities currently? A look at the economic indicators alone reveals a clear polarisation of income in many cities even in wealthy countries, accompanied by an increasing segregation of residents according to their economic situation (Musterd et al. 2015). Some segments of the population simply cannot afford to live in certain neighbourhoods, or even certain cities. Their only option is to use those spaces which are affordable to low-income tenants.

However, the argument about enabling and limiting conditions in a spatial context would not hold if these differences applied only to economic capital, as, following Bourdieu, a wider concept of capital has been used here, tying social advancement to education, taste and social capital. Therefore, a structural disadvantage in the neighbourhood is primarily the result of a lack of access to social and cultural capital. Also, the term milieu itself implies that residents of a neighbourhood share further things in common which constitute their socio-cultural identity (e.g., taste regarding the aesthetics of everyday life, values, consumption preferences).

Contextual and compositional factors play an important role in the constitution of the milieu. At the same time, the residents of a neighbourhood in their action spaces contribute to the constitution of this space.

Löw also supposes "milieu-specific operations of synthesis" that produce the urban space.

But beyond income, education and occupation, which other characteristics apply to a larger number of residents in a neighbourhood?

This question is of central importance for a data-based form of recursive address. If, in addition to economic characteristics, there are further items with a spatial concentration that can be found in the portfolios of data traders, it would follow that the personalised address based on them contributes to the solidification of neighbourhoods. A uniform address with similar financial as well as consumption offers would, over time, contribute to the homogeneity of the population of a neighbourhood. Added to the influence neighbourhood residents have over each other, there is then an externally controlled influence by profit-oriented companies with messages that are related to the dispositions recorded about this locality.

A closer look at the portfolio of data traders could therefore reveal to what extent the captured data reflect the shared characteristics of neighbourhood residents. This goes for economic characteristics, which generally show the degree of socio-spatial segmentation, as well as for further consumption-related characteristics that reflect broader commonalities among the neighbourhood population. In addition to the data collected, it is then of interest by whom and how these data are monetised, as they recursively influence both capital-poor and capital-rich inhabitants.

5.3.1 Acquisition of Data and Procedure

Another large German data trading company is the Bonn-based Nexiga GmbH, which focuses on the monetisation of geo data. It offers site plannings, market analyses and an optimised customer management via the space-related analysis of single characteristics with regard to their distribution, density and combination with other characteristics. Like the other providers mentioned, Nexiga has a large portfolio of stored characteristics on the population, from socio-demographic and economic information to data on sales psychology. The company's market data are composed of more than 280 characteristics with a total of more than 1,000 specifications and can be projected onto different scale levels. In their most detailed resolution, data can be related to individual buildings, of which the company claims to have recorded well over 20 million in Germany alone (www.nexiga.de).

For a neighbourhood-based data analysis, up-to-date data sets for the German cities of Berlin, Munich and Essen were obtained from Nexiga's portfolio in July 2018 and December 2022. Only two criteria guided the selection of these cities: On the one hand, large cities were chosen because neighbourhood formations are more evident there than in small and medium-sized cities. Berlin and Munich are both cities with several million inhabitants and are likely to have a large social spectrum. On the other hand, they were chosen because segregation is not too extreme, making it possible to explore the data economy's reproductive logic in general and independently of already existing polarisations in the social sphere. A study by Helbig and Jähnen (2018) documents an increase in segregation between 2005 and 2014 for Germany's 74 largest cities. Neither Berlin, which is affected by rising rents (17th place in the segregation index), nor Munich, dubbed "Germany's most expensive major city" (61st place), nor Essen, traditionally a dualistic city (25th place), occupy leading positions here (cf. Ibid., p. 30).

The information obtained on the three cities is composed of aggregated data that can be assigned to single street sections as well as data that can be assigned to a neighbourhood. At Nexiga, the neighbourhood level comprises small-scale statistical units, the size of which depends on the number of inhabitants.

At the street section level, several individual data (affinities, indices) with multi-level characteristics were obtained. At the neighbourhood level, a residential environment typology (rating in school grades), information on social class (from lower class to upper class in five levels), income classes (households with monthly net income in five levels) and other neighbourhood-related characteristics are added. The selection thus included characteristics of households that can be combined spatially with social criteria or housing quality. The information was issued as geo data in shapefile format.

The objective is to visualise socio-spatial correlations using various combinations of characteristics at the street and neighbourhood level and to illustrate concentrations of characteristics in an exemplary manner. The key point here is that the data are obtained primarily to gain commercial access to the population in question. Based on the sources of supply described, they provide clues as to where and how the different interests and business models of the data buyers can be realised. They express which segments of the population are being targeted when a particular characteristic they share is relevant for the address. The visualisation of selected features thus selectively reveals exploitation templates to which data buyers recursively refer with their personalised offers.

Admittedly, different resolutions and diverse characteristics can be chosen for this representation of the economic perspective. By aggregating the characteristics at the street segment level, a common form of presentation was chosen that lends itself to an overview of consumers and the living environment of individual cities. Taking up the data set unchanged, among other things, park, water or traffic areas are not shown separately and the area-related feature carriers are not set in relation to the area-related total. The data set centres the frequency of an economically relevant characteristic in a spatial segment. In accordance with the formulated interest in the connection of economic attributions (class, income) with consumption-related characteristics in the neighbourhood context, the corresponding characteristics are illustrated in excerpts, each in pairs.

5.3.2 Berlin, Munich and Essen: Exemplary Attributions in Urban Space

In recent years, **Berlin** has gained nationwide attention as a contested arena of urban displacement and gentrification processes. Due to growing immigration and rising rents, the city is now showing clear signs of segregation. The social transformation of the metropolis picked up speed after the fall of the Wall in the 1990s, when, as a result of delayed structural change, increasing unemployment was registered in the eastern but also in the Western part. Due to the social decline of the laid-off workforce and as a result of growing international immigration and selective mobility processes, a stronger concentration of low-income and educationally disadvantaged segments of the population developed in the urban area. Berlin evolved from a divided city to a "multi-fragmented city" (Krajewski 2015, p. 77). The city's diminishing options for shaping housing policy were exacerbated by the sale of municipal housing units, which was intended to relieve the budget deficit of the debt-ridden metropolis. As a result, private-sector influence on the rental market grew. In addition to privatisation and redevelopment, especially in the areas near the centre of Berlin-Mitte, Berlin's post-Fordist transformation brought about infrastructural improvements in many parts of the city. After years of population stagnation and belated suburbanisation processes on the outskirts of the city with further segregation effects, the economically resurgent city experienced sustained population growth in the years that followed. On average, the city has grown by almost 40,000 inhabitants annually since 2010, which has so far been insufficiently accommodated by new construction (Wetzstein 2018, p. 39f). In addition, the national and international acquisition of real estate has been increasing sharply and, together with a boom in tourism, is exposing residents of centrally located neighbourhoods to growing rental pressure (Holm 2011; Schnur 2013). The trendy neighbourhoods especially, all located in the Wilhelminian Gründerzeit belt, form the centres of a gentrification process that is spreading out from there. Improvements in construction and rent increases then encourage the often-described segregation, in which high-income residents with a specific capital endowment successively spread out at the expense of the less wealthy previous tenants, and the latter have to deal with increasing peripherisation. In Berlin, for example, a stronger spatial concentration of socially disadvantaged segments of the population could be observed from 2010 onward, among others, on the Western outskirts of the city in Spandau and on the eastern outskirts in Marzahn-Hellersdorf (Plate et al. 2014, p. 298f.). If the segregation processes described at the beginning of this study are reflected in Berlin (see, e.g., Holm 2016), it will be interesting to see how the data trade reflects these segregation processes.

We will first take a socio-spatial survey of the data trader as a basis (Fig. 5.1). The data cover a total of 2,168,383 households in Berlin. The area signature is used to highlight all neighbourhoods that have a larger number of lower-class households. Of the available 5 levels of social class, only the lowest level is reflected with the absolute number of households per unit area. At this scale level and taking into account the different reference areas, Berlin presents itself as relatively mixed according to this characteristic. Nevertheless, concentrations of poorer parts of the population can be easily traced via the small-scale dark signatures. In the outer part of the urban area, the large housing estates stand out, such as those found on the above-mentioned city outskirts in Spandau and Marzahn-Hellersdorf. The "Märkische Viertel" in the north and "Gropuisstadt" in the south also stand out. In addition to a clearly discernible share of underclass residents in the Western district of Wilmersdorf, the densely urbanised inner-city belt in particular is characterised by a mosaic of different shades of disadvantaged neighbourhoods. Those neighbourhoods, with their large numbers of low-income residents, would be highly vulnerable in case of further rent increases. By point signature, households with a high affinity for instalment loans are indicated. Of the nine levels between "very low" and "very high" affinity, only the highest level has been selected. All street segments with more than 10% of residents with a very high affinity are marked with dots, which was the case for 404 out of 134,267 street segments.

Clearly, prospective borrowers are heavily concentrated in neighbourhoods with a large number of socially disadvantaged households. A direct address of the neighbourhood residents on the basis of these data could then come from banks, for example, which advertise their financial products in a direct translation of the item. Above, such a typical utilisation context was cited as a reference of a data trader. With regard to the channels described, there are numerous possibilities for making contact: Potential customers can be addressed on the websites they visit, through direct mail or e-mail or collectively. With the clustering of potential

Fig. 5.1 Berlin—Lower class and instalment loans

Fig. 5.2 Berlin—Holders of academic degrees and business magazines

customers in a neighbourhood, a direct mail piece to all residents in that cluster might be a good idea, or neighbourhood-specific billboard advertising might seem appropriate. In other utilisation contexts, an affinity for loans signals a lack of creditworthiness. In combination with other items, this implies excluding neighbourhood residents from targeting with respect to this characteristic. Consequently, customer segmentation selectively interferes in the urban space on the basis of a comprehensive data base, addressing individuals or groups with the offers appropriate for them. As the distributions of the different characteristic bearers clearly show, offers and information reach the inhabitants of Berlin in a highly unequal manner. They correspond with economic status and residential location, making an exchange in these exact social and spatial contexts more likely.

Whether a company can benefit from targeting a spatial segment with an out-of-home campaign, for example, depends on the concentration of the relevant characteristic bearers. Even if a resident does not share the relevant attributes, the fact that he lives in a certain neighbourhood can determine which information and offers he receives. As a result, the recursive reference is not directed specifically at the person but at the feature cluster of a larger section of space.

As their lack of capital is possibly reproduced through specific offers, residents of individual streets or entire neighbourhoods must increasingly deal with offers detrimental to them. At the other end of the spectrum, potential resources reach the privileged segments of the population due to the characteristics recorded about them. Figure 5.2 provides an overview of how academic degree holders are distributed across the city. First of all, the overview reveals that this form of symbolic capital coincides with economic capital in many neighbourhoods. A concentration of holders of academic degrees is clearly visible in the affluent district of Steglitz-Zehlendorf, the districts of Charlottenburg and Westend as well as in the southern parts of the Mitte district. The existence of this category as well will play a role in different utilisation contexts, generally promoting a form of address with further appropriate offers tailored to the educational level.

Superimposing the affinity for business and financial magazines (the highest and second-highest values on the nine-point scale) on top of this plot, shown here in points denoting more than 20% of all households per street segment, again reveals numerous overlaps. As it makes little sense for publishers to invest in contacting populations with no affinity, the identified target group is predestined to receive information with which they can potentially increase their capital. By contrast, the high target group transparency of the data economy prevents the population segments which are not included from obtaining such information. While obtaining this type of information at a later stage is not impossible, it is certainly made less likely, be it via online channels or via addresses in real space.

A closer look at the data for Berlin also reveals that rough interpolations were made for several neighbourhoods (e.g., numerous streets in the Prenzlauer Berg or Tempelhof districts are marked with the same characteristics). Data traders transfer mean values to neighbouring districts, neglecting a more precise description of the target group. Similarly, neighbourhoods that extend across large areas or have a small population are described uniformly on the basis of a small number of feature carriers. The large area at the outskirts of the Western part of Berlin is a good example for this. It includes the Spandauer Forst, which has residential buildings only in its south and east. The overall low social status of its inhabitants is disproportionately represented over the large total area. As a consequence of such generalisations, other people's data can lead to individuals being put at a disadvantage. Conversely, a lack of precision can also mean less rigid personalisation, allowing an individual to receive offers and information not associated with their milieu. Ultimately, each company determines the resolution, the target group accuracy and the quality of the data that it uses to reach its goals.

On the whole, in spite of imprecisions regarding the selected scale levels, patterns are emerging in Berlin's urban space that represent selective targeting of individuals as well as groups of people in the neighbourhood. These patterns are based on personalised data which, through trade and economic valorisation, fortify that which they describe in terms of content and space. The battle over social sovereignty within individual neighbourhoods, as it is currently being waged in Berlin, is thus also related to how a neighbourhood is recursively addressed.

The Bavarian capital of **Munich** has been growing steadily for decades, allowing the city and the region to become one of Europe's most successful locations. The fact that this city is less affected by social polarisation processes than other big cities in Germany is largely owed to its economic structure. The upheaval caused by the structural and social transformation processes of the late 1970s affected Munich to a lesser extent. As Munich was incorporated into Germany's industrialisation and modernisation process fairly late, it succeeded in attracting crisis-resistant high-tech companies which mitigated the decline of the old industries. Until today, the economy in the Munich metropolitan area is characterised by a mix of companies, some of which are interconnected, of different sizes and from a wide range of industries (the so-called Munich Mix). While the city's economic prosperity has positively impacted its job market and also its options regarding social policies, the high cost of living is a big problem for large parts of the population. Already in the 1990s, the Munich Report on Poverty pointed to a rising poverty risk as a result of higher costs of living, a circumstance which the city is still dealing with in the present (Martens 2011, S. 177). Rents, in particular, are placing a growing burden on people's budgets in this rapidly growing city. Similar to Berlin, current challenges for housing policy are linked to the real estate boom in Germany, due to which rental prices have been increasing even more since around 2010. Presently, rents across Munich have become so high that most low-income residents have no choice but to move further and further away from the centre.

Figure 5.3 shows all households which are assigned the worst housing location (level "poor"). In addition, neighbourhoods are highlighted in which a larger number of residents is considered to belong to the lower class. Overall, the data include 813,491 households. Both characteristics reflect a relatively balanced socio-spatial distribution and correlate only to a limited extent. A poor residential location cannot be applied to larger neighbourhoods across the board; rather, it is heavily trafficked streets, especially arterial roads and parts of the Mittlerer Ring, that stand out as disadvantaged residential locations. Households that form part of the lower class are equally divided across different urban areas. Nevertheless, Munich also has neighbourhoods where poor residential location and a high number of lower-class households coincide, such as the districts of Hasenbergl and Am Hart, which are characterised by larger apartment blocks. Like in other disadvantaged neighbourhoods, residents are faced with various location-related disadvantages, such as those described above. With respect to the contextual factors, the material equipment as well as the symbolic connotations of a place are to be emphasised. Hasenbergl in particular has over the decades become known as Munich's problem neighbourhood. The negative connotations of the neighbourhood can have a detrimental effect on residents' self-esteem, and the stigma associated with it can put them at a disadvantage in professional and everyday life.

With the intelligence collected by the data-processing service providers, discriminating targeting becomes systemic: Companies offering exclusive goods or advertise certain cultural events or even such that take place elsewhere will hardly target any of the residents of such a neighbourhood as they do not see a market here. Consequently, the corresponding content does not become part of the socialisation context or neighbourhood exchange. Class-specific habitualisations are challenged by external offers to a lesser extent and social advancement is made more difficult.

To trace the selective targeting of neighbourhood residents in more detail, we will take a more differentiated look at a section in Munich's southeast, specifically the neighbourhoods of the Ramersdorf district and the Neuperlach district (Fig. 5.4). The core of eastern Ramersdorf is an established single-family housing development with middle-class residents, which in the map section only changes to a multi-story row house area with a larger number of social housing units in the south up to

5 DECONTEXTUALISED DATA AND SOCIO-SPATIAL … 123

Fig. 5.3 Munich—Lower class and quality of residential location

Ständlerstraße. Connected to the east by the Ostpark is Neuperlach, one of the largest post-war housing projects in West Germany. Neuperlach was erected in the 1960s and 70s as an extensive large housing estate to meet the rapidly growing demand for housing in Munich at the time. Originally built for middle-class residents, Neuperlach has today become one of Munich's poorer districts. In a citywide comparison, the social indicators reveal higher scores with regard to poverty density and receipt of government support (Stadt München 2017). Although the social differences between the neighbourhoods are relativised in the overall social spectrum of Munich, the neighbourhood structure still points to different socialisation contexts within a distance of only a few 100 meters. The residents of northern Ramersdorf have relatively large, individually different house and living spaces as well as their own use of gardens. The neighbourhood has facilities such as a restaurant, a bakery, clothing stores, a Montessori preschool and a centrally located park which foster contact between residents. In contrast, Neuperlach's large housing estate is characterised by standardised construction, offering considerably less room for individuality. For shopping and leisure activities, residents only have the estate's central facilities. Furthermore, both neighbourhoods belong to different school districts, which means that the children do not have a chance to come into contact with each other during school. While Munich's southwest is generally wealthy, it can be divided into different areas of acquisition for the population. While upper-class neighbourhoods further away (such as Nymphenburg or the suburb of Grünwald) are certainly characterised by a higher degree of social distance, even in a small geographic area there are clear differences regarding the conditions for the acquisition of capital and the above-mentioned barriers regarding access, perception and social exclusion.

With regard to the external influence of data traders the question is whether these small-scale differences between Ramersdorf and Neuperlach show up in the provider's portfolio. As an example, the purchasing power beyond the Munich average (index value > 125) and concern for the environment is shown in its effect on consumer behaviour. While the purchasing power relevant for the sale of products is exists in some of Neuperlach's households, the potential sales area is diminished by other characteristics, such as concern for the environment. A marked concern on the part of the residents of eastern Ramersdorf stands in stark contrast to the neighbouring residents, with clear consequences for the targeting. As a consequence, offers and information related to the environment are more likely to reach eastern Ramersdorf, providing content for everyday activities and social exchange.

Since the data-based selection is derived from personalised information, commercial addresses always include messages related to this information. In relation to a neighbourhood, however, this does not mean that a campaign will be addressed exclusively to that neighbourhood. Companies aiming to place a specific ad, a credit offer or an insurance policy will also consider characteristics relevant that are present across spaces and milieus. In the end, the provider's goal is to maximise customer potential. Numerous characteristics, such as "gender", "customer card user", affinity for home delivery food" or "distrustful financial client", which are offered by Nexiga for target group segmentation are not attributable to an economic status. The available diversity of characteristics, which affects rich and poor residents alike, could result in a targeting that provides disadvantaged segments of the population with the same content that

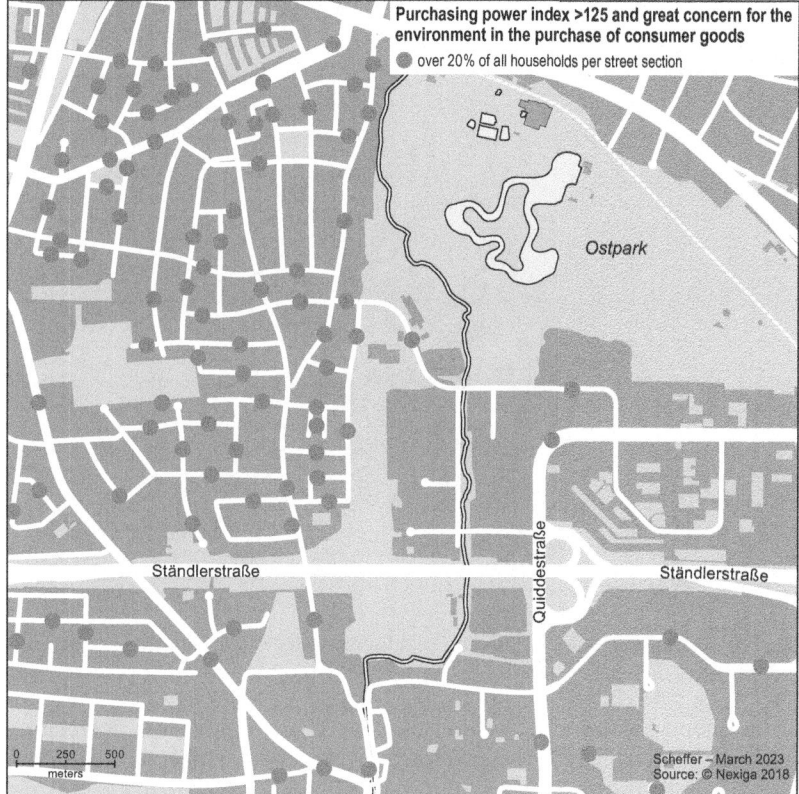

Fig. 5.4 Munich, Ramersdorf-Perlach—Purchasing power index and concern for the environment

wealthier households also receive. In other words: With reference to items that apply to all milieus, the argument of recursive targeting could be countered. The characteristics that are then relevant in this context are the ones which allow access to services and goods with which their recipients can successfully engage in processes of distinction. One such characteristic could be "significance of product novelty".

Figure 5.5 shows the highest value for the attitude "The product novelty/innovation factor is decisive when buying consumer goods" (the highest and second-highest values on the nine-point scale) and

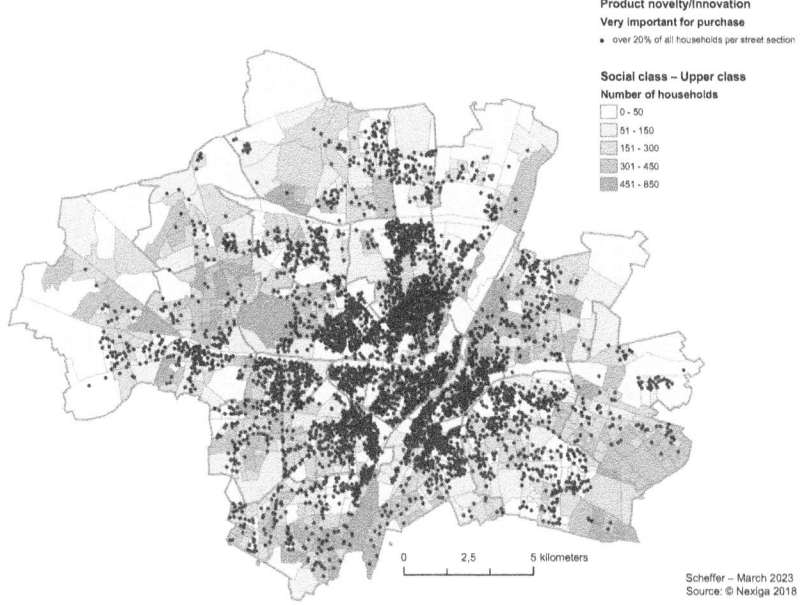

Fig. 5.5 Munich—Upper class and product novelty

the frequency of upper-class households. There is no clear correlation between the two characteristics. However, an accumulation regarding this interest stands out in the city centre, even if one takes into account the relatively higher density of settlement in the Gründerzeit neighbourhoods close to the city centre. The interest in product novelty may partly coincide with the spatial distribution of younger urban residents, for whom the desire for an urban environment in a central location is particularly important. Even if this again means a disproportional representation of expensive and prestigious districts such as Schwabing-West, Maxvorstadt or Au-Haidhausen, inhabitants lacking capital are also linked to attributions that carry distinctions in this example. A discriminating form of address again comes into play when cross-milieu characteristics are combined with other characteristics in data processing. Someone who markets an expensive watch, for example, will want more than a target group that appreciates the novelty of the product. To minimise wastage, the addressed target group should above all be able to pay for the watch.

Similarly, a basic "affinity for home delivery food" or a "distrusting financial customer" still results in a fuzzy customer profile, the specification of which can be achieved precisely via additional economic characteristics. Last but not least, the widespread use of predefined milieu classifications (Sinus milieus, Geo milieus) underscores the high relevance of economic capital in the data traders' portfolio.

The comparison of the Hasenbergl/Am Hart district and the expensive Bogenhausen district (Fig. 5.6) shows how the affinity for new products changes when economic criteria, such as the affinity for instalment loans, are considered: Both have high percentages of residents receptive to new, innovative products per street segment (highest and second highest on the nine-point scale). However, if only customers with no interest in instalment loans are considered (also the highest and second-highest score on the nine-point scale), a provider will direct his offers almost exclusively to Bogenhausen.

Another argument against the social bridging function of cross-milieu items lies in the diversity of address. By using personal data to present the customer with ever-new commercial messages, he is confronted with his own dispositions in a variety of ways. Overall, a highly individual form of acquisition must be assumed which distinguishes between residents of a neighbourhood in many respects. This does certainly not imply social change. If the existing dispositions of every individual are mirrored, the same is true for the population of a neighbourhood. The influence coming from the outside may have a less homogenising effect on the social conditions, but what reaches an individual in various combinations is again a reflection of individual dispositions.

Munich as a city less segregated than others is affected by such a stabilisation of existing social conditions through a reflexive form of address just as much as other cities.

As a former centre of the German coal and steel industry, **Essen** is fundamentally different from the above-mentioned cities in its economic development and socio-spatial structure. The city's boom during industrialisation ended with the decline of mining in the late 1950s. The long-term structural crisis led to a significant decline of the population since 1965. Not until 2012 did the city again record a population increase. Essen's socio-spatial structure is directly linked to the development of mining: The more densely built-up north, with numerous working-class neighbourhoods in former coal-mining areas, was directly affected by the northward migration of mining and by the crisis in coal

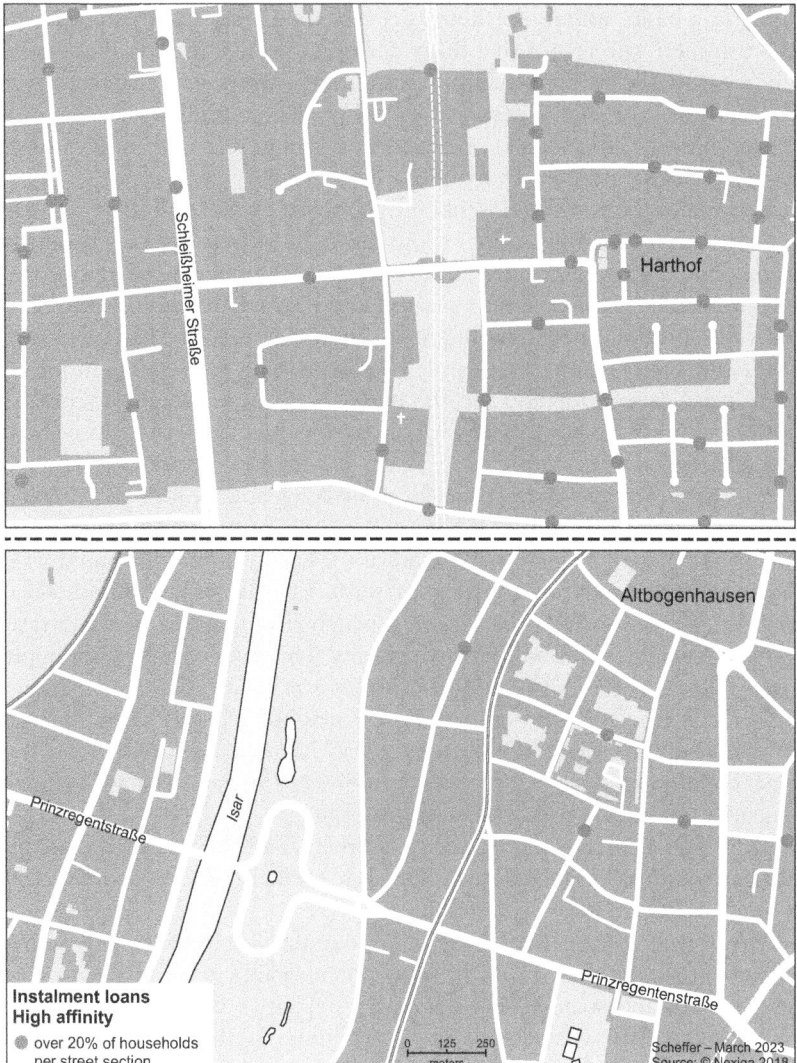

Fig. 5.6 Munich—Product novelty and instalment loans in a comparison of neighbourhoods

and steel, while the south established itself as the preferred residential area of industrialists and other wealthy sections of the population. A few exceptions apart, Essen's north has long been characterised by a disproportionately high number of welfare recipients and a high proportion of immigrants (Grabbert 2008, S. 139ff). By contrast, the south of Essen has only a low number of low-income residents. This inequality of opportunity is reflected in the field of education, among others. In the north, a comparatively low percentage of students attends a school that prepares them for university, while the numerically smaller number of children from the south mostly do their *Abitur* (the prerequisite for studying at a university) (Strohmeier 2006, S. 13). In recent years, a gradient between outside and inside has been added to Essen's polarised spatial structure. Some neighbourhoods on the outskirts of the northern city area show signs of structural upgrading. By contrast, the northern belt of the city centre, with its post-war apartment buildings, is one of the city's main areas in need of development.

Essen's large-scale polarisation is clearly reflected in the traded geo data, which includes 312,439 households. Households with a "good" or "very good" residential location are located in the neighbourhoods that also have the highest number of upper-class households (Fig. 5.7). While few upper-class households can be found in Essen's north, the south has a high concentration of wealthy residents. The discrepancy between inside and outside mentioned above is reflected particularly in the concentration of upper-class households in the northwest, where the neighbourhoods of Frintrop and Gerschede also have a very high-quality residential location. In comparison, the centre of Essen is characterised by areas with a low number of upper-class households.

The map clearly reflects residential location and social class even in small-scale concentration; a notable cluster of upper-class households is always tied to a privileged residential location. Essen is a prime example of the congruence between social and spatial inequality, at the same time pointing to the socially reproductive effect associated with the social, symbolic and material dimensions of the neighbourhood.

Their causes can be traced back historically in a relational perspective to, among other things, the powerful constitution of space by the mine operators and the economically justified arrangement of infrastructure and workers' settlements. Numerous external actors are also involved in the institutionalised space of the mining industry, for example, as buyers of

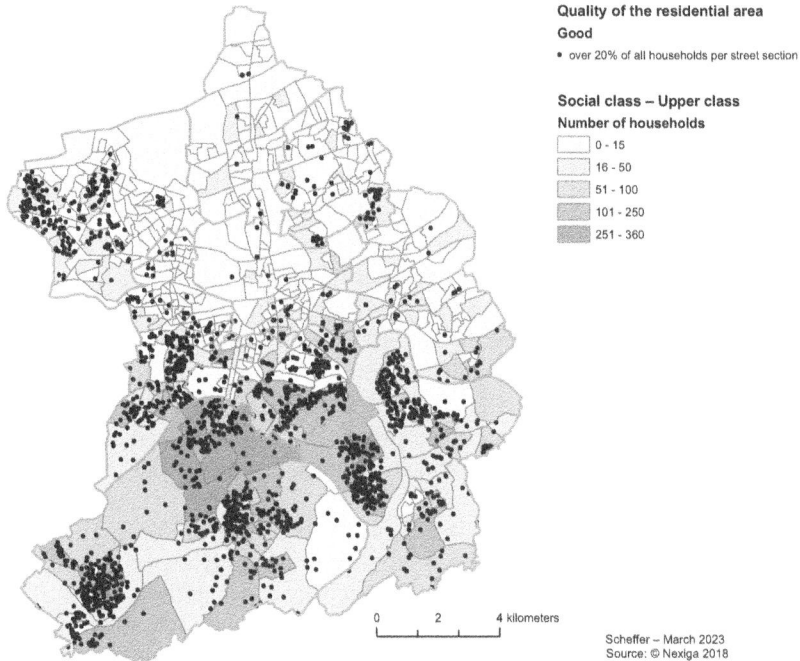

Fig. 5.7 Essen—Upper class and quality of the residential area

raw materials, who later, through their reduced demand, contributed to the industrial area's decline.

To conclude, we will once again relate the polarised social structure to the selective targeting of the data-processing economy. Analogous to the cluster of upper-class households, Essen's lower-class households are shown in their spatial distribution. They are combined here with "affinity for TV shopping" (highest and second-highest values on the nine-point scale) (Fig. 5.8). By way of example, the distribution of the characteristic carriers again points to the spatial connection between economic and consumption-related characteristics. The affinity for TV shopping can be found almost exclusively in Essen's north with its prevalence of lower-class milieus. More than 1,000 households here are considered to be receptive to TV targeting, a result that is certainly relevant for many businesses interested in individual forms of address. Via smart TV, this demand can

5 DECONTEXTUALISED DATA AND SOCIO-SPATIAL ...   131

be met in an increasingly personalised manner. Conversely, a higher relevance of TV consumption and the messages from advertising feed into consumer socialisation. Unless mobile platforms are used, this way of obtaining what one needs ties consumers to their homes, replacing trips to the places that are in demand across milieus. Over the long term, such places and their resources disappear, as perception becomes more and more habitualised. The forms of social recognition including the possibilities of distinction from the products obtained via TV shopping take place exclusively within the milieu.

Superimposing the slides shown with their attributions of the population, the selection made already reveals a system of utilisation that reproduces inequality. This happens within cities via the unequal allocation of information and services, which were diagnosed above as resources for capital acquisition. The unequal allocation takes place at different scale

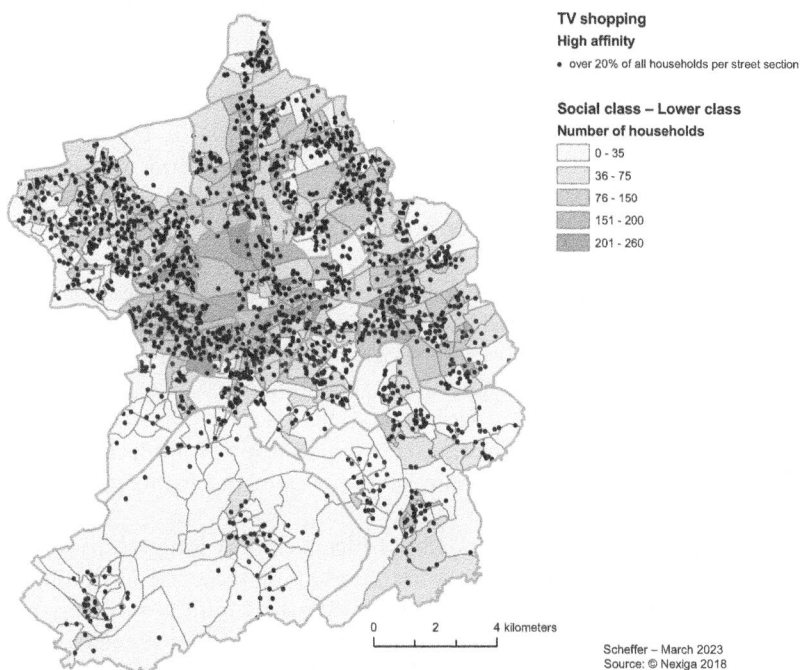

Fig. 5.8   Essen—Lower class and TV shopping

levels according to economic selection criteria and has the potential of social entrenchment.

So far, references to space and neighbourhoods have been made deliberately, although the traded data can reach individuals also outside of their place of residence. In addition, the data feed into other utilisation contexts directed at the neighbourhood, influencing opportunity structures there.

5.3.3 *Externally Driven Site Effects*

The campaigns mentioned target individual or collective attributions from which those interests and needs are sifted out which the business exploiting the data can meet with specific products and services. In addition to this usage which involves a direct address of the relevant feature carriers, there are other forms of data utilisation. Product providers can use the transparency of a city's inhabitants to align their local presence with the customer.

Let us return to the findings on Munich's southeast, which revealed an increased demand for organic products in eastern Ramersdorf and a lower demand in the adjacent neighbourhood of Neuperlach. For someone planning to open a new store based on these criteria and in search of the right location, such comparisons are crucial. Thanks to the extensive database, the sales and customer potential, frequencies, market environment, accessibility, consumer and residential typology, product-specific purchasing power or competing locations can all be analysed for each location planning, as offered for instance by Nexiga. Nexiga refers to its own case study on an organic supermarket, for which the company analysed, among other characteristics, the number of households with the "environmental" consumption style, retail-relevant purchasing power and age groups (https://www.nexiga.com/?s=Case+Study). This helps the respective provider to estimate which investments are worthwhile in which neighbourhoods.

For neighbourhood residents, this results in a utility infrastructure with placements and orientations that are a result of recorded attributions. While purchasing power may only influence the number of shops, the translation of consumption preferences contributes to a greater differentiation of living contexts. Milieus with high levels of education and capital can expect a different supply structure in their neighbourhoods than socially disadvantaged ones. Citing Bourdieu, the ruling class's "taste for luxury" could be contrasted with the lower class's "taste for necessity". Interestingly, the different supply structures do not result primarily from the actions of the neighbourhood residents, but from the decision of businesses operators, who create personalised spaces based on a comprehensive database. What Bourdieu failed to see is a constitution of space that comes before actions and practices of distinction, in this case resulting from the rational calculations of a data-based site planning.

This externally driven design of space can have far-reaching consequences: Based on the products of data trader Nexiga, site planning involves optimising all operational processes, selecting suitable territories and sites according to sales potential or identifying suitable personnel. In addition, the neighbourhood residents' numerous items can be used to align products, prices and assortments with regional and local needs as well. What the data economy does is thus nothing less than providing an opportunity to rationally shape space in those areas that are not regulated by the public sector. Even if this implementation is gradual, many data-based decisions do not necessarily have anything to do with personalised dispositions and persistent structures are constraining it, a growing impact on the neighbourhood must be considered.

If this form of spatial constitution is viewed as a socialisation context, we are again facing the problem of inequality of opportunity, in this case dependent on the neighbourhood. As has been shown for Berlin, Munich and Essen, in each case a different social spectrum results in spatial structures which provide unequal resources. In an extreme case, on one end of the spectrum we find a spatial structure that provides its distinguished residents with rare and expensive goods, supporting them in their practices of distinction. This is taking place in an exclusive sales environment, which at the other end of the spectrum is contrasted with a low-priced standard range in simple stores or discounters. Even when the differences are less pronounced, it is evident that the lifelong experiences in these environments shape young people for different life paths. In the first case, clear opportunities exist to increase the cultural, social and symbolic capital, while in the second case, there are hardly any guidelines for connecting to the rules, codes and manners of the privileged class. The private-sector's interest in a profitable spatial design produces new site effects.

Data-based constitution of space reveals another form of recursive acquisition. While so far freely traded data in the different forms of their capitalisation represented a direct form of recursive address, it is now the transformation into spatial structures which reaches the consumer recursively in an indirect form. The neighbourhood is constituted through corporate action, expressing inhabitants' dispositions within an economically relevant segment of space. By mirroring the dispositions of the spatial segment it creates a recursive acquisition.

To summarise, it is evident that real-space structures do not necessarily need a technological infrastructure with sensors, cameras and displays to reflect social conditions based on data. Added to the types of recursive acquisition, as illustrated by numerous examples covering all basic functions of existence as well as in the context of the sentient city, there is the indirect effect of a commercial infrastructure. Mixed forms of such data-based spaces are also conceivable, as for example when a supermarket uses personalised data both for site planning and for ads on their own customer displays. Clearly, we are dealing with different contexts which, in addition to virtual forms of personalised influence, also have an effect in physical real space. In view of growing data markets, which are able to guarantee economic success through customer transparency more and more convincingly, further translations of individual characteristics into commercial offers are to be expected. Economic actors are indirectly perpetuating social inequality.

5.4 Interim Conclusion: Bourdieu in the Context of the Data Economy

Commercial data trading has a strong social influence, which is not based on the data traders' privilege to alone cover the need for personalised data. As has been shown, a targeted capturing of data is now taking place in many different contexts, and they are passed on in various forms outside of the official markets. What is remarkable, however, is that it is data trade that can systematically externalise in aggregated and economically processed form all that has accumulated about individuals in a wide variety of contexts by means of modern information and communication technologies. Increasing transparency of the target person can be achieved in a planned manner through data trading from manifold sources and can be put into value economically.

The data subjects themselves hardly have an economic benefit as a result of this cross-space trade. But since the characteristics that are traded are immaterial, the loss remains abstract. It becomes concrete, however, when the ways of monetisation are analysed.

The form of analysis chosen here focuses on the major data traders in Germany. Their comprehensive portfolio first of all testifies to the commercial significance of the data in general. For an interpretation focused on social stratification processes, the way they are used is also instructive: The customer can be reached through numerous channels via cyberspace or real space by linking the respective information, service or product offer with the stored characteristics of the target person. Familiar and fitting messages are recombined economically and brought to the customer recursively. According to Bourdieu, the milieu-specific acquisition of knowledge, taste or culture contains the reflexive element which consolidates the habitus, reducing the chances to advance to other milieus. Correspondingly, the recursive adoption of habitualised characterisations by data buyers, transmitted by personalised messages and appropriated via products, information and services, must be understood as a barrier to advancement.

Bourdieu tied social positions that people occupy in social space depending on their capital to lifestyles, relating consumption and leisure preferences, occupations and income to each other (Bourdieu 1984, S. 262f). The different indicators used for the classification of milieus now appear in the data traders' portfolio in a greatly expanded form. A wide range of information with detailed subdivisions is available on large parts of the population—in some cases even in real time. With this information, it is possible to differentiate groups in a more refined and comprehensive way than Bourdieu was ever able to do in his empirical studies in France.

At a superficial glance, this finding could be taken as an argument for a far-reaching differentiation of society, in which social differences are blurred by the diversity of available lifestyles despite unequal capital endowments. In this view, an enormous range of features could be combined with an enormous variety of offers.

In the hands of data traders and their customers, however, attributions represent the possibility of deliberately moderating the fundamentally free choice of lifestyle. In partly automated allocations, content is directly linked to existing preferences, while the range of interests that are addressed often depend on the economic capital. This characteristic, which is a central component of almost all offers and typologies, makes it possible for the provider to assess the ability to pay and to offer a more differentiated service according to the interests recorded.

While Bourdieu might find it more difficult today to distinguish lifestyles and social positions by means of distinctive characteristics, there is much to be said for the fact that addressing each individual in a precisely tailored way systematically counteracts a differentiation that is independent of class. The heterogeneity of the target groups can be managed by flexible combinations of the richly available data, hampering social change.

From a spatial perspective, the reproductive logic must be particularly evident if a data-based approach also reaches the majority of neighbourhood residents. Then, the "mirroring" of that which is one's own is supplemented by a one-sided address of the neighbourhood. A closer look at commercially offered geo data reveals exactly this influence on the different neighbourhoods of Berlin, Munich and Essen, among others. Depending on the available income, population groups are not only distributed differently across the urban area, they also sometimes show similar affinities in their respective clusters. Thus, the selective targeting of individual population groups reproduces their neighbourhoods beyond economic characteristics.

Since the economic circumstances of neighbourhood residents often play a special role in practice, as is clearly demonstrated by almost all of the data traders' reference projects, economic criteria come into play again and again as a principle for structuring customer groups. As an example from Munich Bogenhausen in comparison with Hasenbergl/Am Hart illustrates, the neighbourhoods relevant for the address can then be grouped together even more closely via the material dimension.

In addition to the various selection processes used by companies to narrow down target groups for direct contact, there are also selections for location and sales planning. The supply intended for each population segment, such as supermarket offering certain products, is again based on economic possibilities and other preferences, which are expressed physically, resulting in overarching (dis)advantages as a result of how spaces are equipped.

Bourdieu (especially 1991) is always guided by the actions of the privileged who take possession of a space and also occupy it symbolically. Under the data economy, however, the different spatial profits also result from the data-based decisions of businesses, whose sole focus is on the distribution of market-relevant actors in the urban space. In combination with the different ways of directing messages at each target group, they have a reinforcing effect on social milieus in space. Paradoxically, this is taking place under the technological conditions of the digital age, once praised as an opportunity to overcome social stratification processes.

References

Acquisti, Alessandro; John, Leslie K. & Loewenstein, George (2013): What Is Privacy Worth? In: The Journal of Legal Studies 42 (2), 249–274.
Bourdieu, Pierre (1984): *Distinction. A Social Critique of the Judgement of Taste.* New York, London: Routledge.
Federal Trade Commission (2014): *Data Brokers. A Call for Transparency and Accountability.* Washington.
Goldhammer, Klaus & Wiegand, André (2017): Ökonomischer Wert von Verbraucherdaten für Adress- und Datenhändler. Goldmedia GmbH Strategy Consulting. Berlin. Online: https://www.bmj.de/SharedDocs/Downloads/DE/PDF/Berichte/Oekon_Wert_Daten_Adresshaendler.pdf?__blob=publicationFile (01.03.2023)
Grabbert, Tammo (2008): *Schrumpfende Städte und Segregation. Eine vergleichende Studie über Leipzig und Essen.* Berlin: Wissenschaftlicher Verlag.
Helbig, Marcel & Jähnen, Stefanie (2018): Wie brüchig ist die soziale Architektur unserer Städte? Trends und Analysen der Segregation in 74 deutschen Städten. Wissenschaftszentrum Berlin für Sozialforschung GmbH. Berlin. Online: https://www.econstor.eu/handle/10419/179001 (01.03.2023)
Holm, Andrej (2011): Kosten der Unterkunft als Segregationsmotor. Befunde aus Berlin und Oldenburg. *Informationen zur Raumentwicklung* (9), 557–566.
Holm, Andrej (2016): Gentrification und das Ende der Berliner Mischung. In: Eberhard von Einem (ed.): *Wohnen.* Wiesbaden: Springer, 191–231.
Hotho, Andreas; Pedersen, Rasmus Ulslev & Wurst, Michael (2010): Ubiquitous Data. In: Michael May & Lorenza Saitta (eds.): *Ubiquitous Knowledge Discovery.* Berlin, Heidelberg: Springer, 61–74.
Krajewski, Christian (2015): Arm, sexy und immer teurer. Standort 39 (2-3), 77–85.
Martens, Rudolf (2011): Armutsberichterstattung und Regelsatzanpassung für Ballungsräume: das Beispiel München. In: Bernd Belina, Norbert Gestring, Wolfgang Müller & Detlev Sträter (eds.): *Urbane Differenzen. Disparitäten innerhalb und zwischen Städten.* Münster: Westfälisches Dampfboot, 163–183.
Musterd, Sako; Tammaru, Tiit; Marcinczak, Szymon & van Ham, Maarten (eds.) (2015): *Socio-Economic Segregation in European Capital Cities: East Meets West.* Milton Park: Taylor and Francis.
Pentland, Alex; Lipton, Alexander & Hardjono, Thomas (2021): *Building the New Economy: Data As Capital.* Cambridge, MIT Press.

Plate, Elke; Polinna, Cordelia & Tonndorf, Thorsten (2014): Aufwertung. Verdrängung. Soziale Mischung sichern. Das Beispiel Berlin. *Informationen zur Raumentwicklung* (4), 291–304.
Schnur, Olaf (2013): Zwischen Stigma, Subvention und Selbstverantwortung. Ambivalenzen der Quartiersentwicklung in Berlin. *Geographische Rundschau* 65 (2), 28–36.
Stadt München (2017): Regionaler Sozialatlas München. Online: http://mstatistik-muenchen.de/regionalersozialatlas/2017/atlas.html.
Strohmeier, Klaus Peter (2006): Segregation in den Städten. Bonn: Friedrich-Ebert-Stiftung Abt. Wirtschafts- und Sozialpolitik (Gesprächskreis Migration und Integration). Online: http://library.fes.de/pdf-files/asfo/04168.pdf. (01.03.2023)
Wetzstein, Steffen (2018): Bezahlbares städtisches Wohnen im internationalen Vergleich. *Informationen zur Raumentwicklung* (4), 34–47.
Wiewiorra, Lukas (2018): Transparenz und Kontrolle in der Datenökonomie. *Wirtschaftsdienst* (7), 463–466.

Open Access This chapter is licensed under the terms of the Creative Commons Attribution 4.0 International License (http://creativecommons.org/licenses/by/4.0/), which permits use, sharing, adaptation, distribution and reproduction in any medium or format, as long as you give appropriate credit to the original author(s) and the source, provide a link to the Creative Commons license and indicate if changes were made.

The images or other third party material in this chapter are included in the chapter's Creative Commons license, unless indicated otherwise in a credit line to the material. If material is not included in the chapter's Creative Commons license and your intended use is not permitted by statutory regulation or exceeds the permitted use, you will need to obtain permission directly from the copyright holder.

CHAPTER 6

Recursive Spaces—Conclusion and Outlook

Abstract This final chapter sums up the mechanisms of social stabilisation using a summary diagram, clearly highlighting again the three types of social reproduction ("ternary recursivity") in the digital age presented in the study. The outlook summarises the changing spatial structures and raises the following question: Which strategies and demands could the identified losers of the digital transformation use for their purposes in a situation where their opportunity for social advancement is increasingly curtailed by the data economy?

Keywords Mirrored spaces · Recursive spaces · Digital empowerment · Social question

The economic opportunities to profit from data-based knowledge are manifold. Academic research and reflection about the long-term consequences of the data economy on social structures are urgently needed.

In the eyes of many critics, digital processing technologies can be understood as the vanguard of a disruptive process that is increasingly fuelled by the commercial exploitation of customer transparency. According to Betancourt (2016), for example, what is emerging in digital capitalism is a valorisation of the individual and their social background. Automated systems constantly interfere in life with offers and services, controlling it to maximise the profits of their creators. In this society of transparency, we are faced with a digital colonisation of the personal (cf. also Han 2013; Zuboff 2015). Such interpretations nonwithstanding, a far-reaching metrisation has already become part of everyday life (Lupton 2016; Kropf and Laser 2019). Practices of measuring, categorising and evaluating of the social characterise numerous new business fields or can be described as conditions of individual competitiveness in traditional business fields. Looking at the networked products and digital services, it is apparent that there are very few technological innovations that benefit only the user. In almost every case, the technology is also able to change the direction of the data flow to turn personal information into something that can be exploited economically. This change of direction shifts the power of action from the user to the provider, whose personalised practices of exploitation are accompanied by considerable regulations. These consequences of digitalisation have not yet been examined in relation to the social question. Disadvantaged segments of the population are being addressed selectively, and instead of resources that could help them to advance socially, they are presented with the known and familiar. Registered and prescribed preferences create mirror cabinets where existing social conditions are reproduced.

The implications for society of this process are made particularly apparent in a spatial perspective: On the one hand, the unequal opportunity structure of physical real space perpetuates social inequality. Following a relational understanding of space, this inequality is produced ongoingly with the disadvantaged parts of the population having less influence on the constitution of space than those with resources at their disposal. Inequality results from the unequal ability to constitute space. Based on this diagnosis, the rules of what is possible, the filters, grids, distances and distinction practices can be fully understood.

On the other hand, it has been shown that the technical preconditions of social influence can be studied in a differentiated manner in spatial contexts. The embedding of sensors in urban spaces, the integration of smart technologies along individual action spaces and the exact recording of actions in shops becomes tangible and analysable on different spatial scale levels. The same is true for the various contexts of personalised targeting. And it is true for cyberspace, which in most areas is also set up with the purpose of data exploitation, addressing the user in the most systematic way possible. In this sense, space provides a structure that is influenced in unequal ways with the help of technology and that in turn addresses individuals in unequal ways, in the form of real space or cyberspace.

All of these processes have recursive mechanisms built into them which make it difficult for milieus lacking in resources to advance socially. This final chapter presents a diagram to summarise and review the social mechanisms of perpetuation, once again highlighting the three forms of social reproduction ("ternary recursivity") in the digital age. In the outlook, the changing spatial structures will be summarised, addressing the question of which strategies and demands the identified losers of the digital transformation could use when the data economy increasingly curtails their opportunities to advance in society.

6.1 Ternary Recursivity

Socialisation in real space as a learning and internalisation process mediated by society is determined by a person's social and physical environment. The increasing polarisation of (urban) social spaces is likely to lead to a polarisation of these socialisation influences as well. Opportunities for social contact, educational institutions, leisure activities, mobility options, a neighbourhood's image, etc., provide a higher potential for capital acquisition or reduce this potential in places where they do not exist. Together, these factors create feedback loops, resulting in an increasing homogeneity of spaces with accessible options on the one hand and limiting restrictions on the other. Because of these restrictions, access to all the world's knowledge, products and services is limited by the filters of habitual, milieu-specific dispositions. This limitation primarily refers not to the quantity of goods and offers, which can usually be found in less privileged spaces, but particularly to the quality of those offers that are conducive to social advancement. This is the *first recursive element* of space as material and social environment, as the structure of its offers correlates with the available capital and the habitus. The more outside influences sort populations, the quality of neighbourhoods or leisure infrastructures based on social criteria as a result of a market logic, the more unequal the division of opportunities in space is. Current processes of displacement due to housing shortage, the international real estate market's luxury homes addressed to wealthy customers, a gastronomy and leisure industry geared to specialised demand or urban upgrading measures in the context of a global competition between cities, all have a huge effect on the opportunity structure of individual residents.

These social mechanisms of exclusion and demarcation of milieus, as well as different practices of distinction and the meanings of types of capital can be analysed with Bourdieu´s site effects. However, since Bourdieu puts societal processes above physical space, completely excluding technical as well as supra-local factors of influence, his analysis tools are limited. These shortcomings have been repeatedly criticised in recent discussions of Bourdieu (Lamont et al. 2015). They become particularly apparent when the focus lies on the process of space creation, as done by Martina Löw (2016). As a "relational arrangement of living beings and social goods", space is constituted by spacing and synthesis performance. By contrast, Bourdieu´s concept of space (in addition to the purely metaphorical "social space") is rigid and social processes are merely inscribed into it. As a result, he is forced to leave out a *second recursive element*, which is the habitus-bound and resource-dependent ability of each individual to influence spatial conditions. While actors with a lot of capital can constitute space in a manner that benefits their social positioning, the segments of the population lacking in capital have less potential to improve their social position through spatial arrangements. Here as well, the specific perception ("synthesis performance") influences the scope of options and, as with Bourdieu, is related to the internalised social order. What is missing in Löw´s relational concept of space is a deeper look at the space-constituting forces of the market economy in relation to the social question. In fact, the described inequality of the opportunity structure can be analysed particularly well in the context of an economic exploitation of space by powerful actors. Following economic principles, spacing takes effect on different spatial levels, creating barriers and social distance. This happens especially where there is a demand for social homogeneity or even exclusivity. Luxury travel destinations, exclusive hotel lobbies, fancy restaurants or gated communities are extreme examples of such a demand. These institutional arrangements, which perpetuate inequality through the polarisation of resources, also involve supra-regional actors. They make it even harder for populations lacking in capital to identify the causes of the discriminating structures.

In summary, physical accessibility, habitualised perception and social accessibility can be understood as socially stratifying mechanisms which have a strong effect in real space. If we succeeded in reducing this impact in cyberspace through new forms of accessibility, digital technologies would have an enormous potential for social empowerment, and there are cases where they actually do. For instance, the socially stratifying rules of real space can be overcome through virtual spaces of interaction where social and cultural capital can be shared. However, this acquisition of resources still needs to have an effect in real space.

Experts in socialisation and education view the unequal opportunities to obtain digital content as another limitation. In addition to availability, they mainly point out the unequal use of cyberspace: Once again, real-space socialisation, habits and an unequal capital endowment prestructure the access to digital offers. These obstacles, often referred to as digital divides, seem to indicate that social inequality can be overcome only with the help of digital technologies: The task of policymakers then lies solely in providing the technical infrastructure and end devices as well as in helping users to obtain digital resources across social classes.

However, this completely ignores the fact that obtaining digital technologies comes at the cost of far-reaching measuring practices, and it is precisely these costs that run counter to the goal of equal participation. This measuring provides businesses with personal data which are exploited economically in a way that cements existing social conditions. In this process we can find the *third recursive element*, which has been the main focus of this work.

In Fig. 6.1, the individual is positioned between real space and cyberspace with his or her individual pattern of perception, thought and action (habitus) and capital endowment (resources). In the age of digitalisation, both spaces influence socialisation, both offer resources (contacts, education, information) that can facilitate social advancement. An individual can "enter" cyberspace and real space simultaneously, as they physically remain in real space even while on the internet, playing an online game or using a virtual reality application. At the same time, both spaces intersect in cases where, for example, digital technologies are embedded in real space (Internet of Things, smart cities) or real-space representations are mediated digitally (augmented reality).

A relational concept of space can be transferred to both spaces. Through actions and perceptions, structures are constituted as arrangements in real space just as they are in cyberspace. However, there is a fundamental difference: The "duality of space" stressed by Löw, which transports the interaction between action and structure to space, is valid for cyberspace only to a limited extent. From real space, cyberspace can be constituted independently, and it is not determined by the structures of cyberspace itself. This means that in the virtual sphere, structure and action can be related to each other only to a limited extent. At the

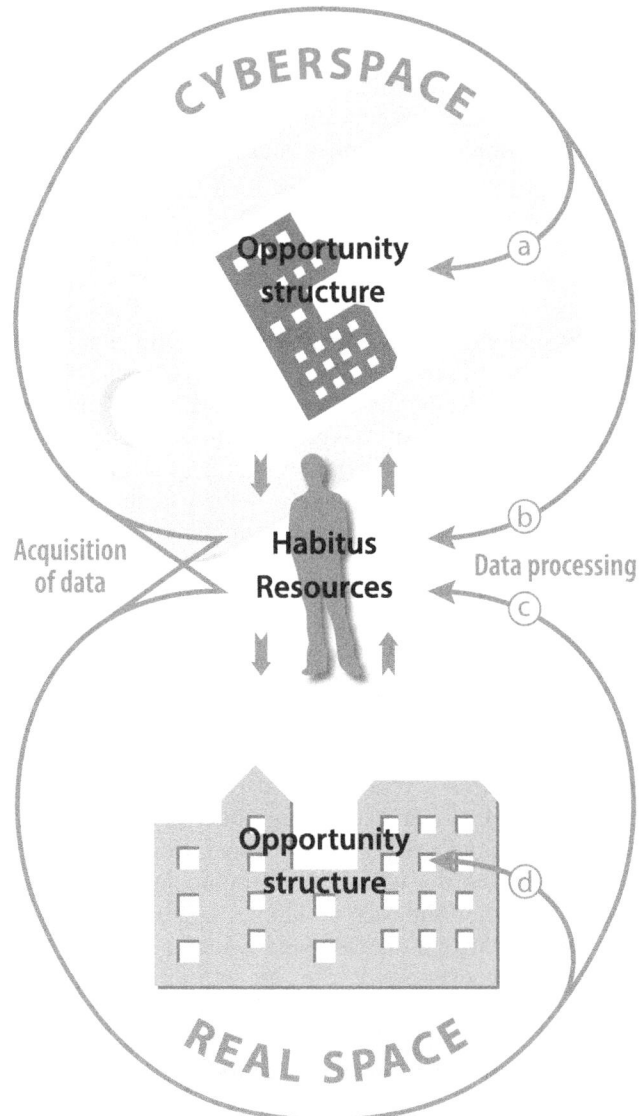

Fig. 6.1 Types of recursive address (a–d)

same time, the respective rules of the constitution of space differ from each other. In real space, spacing takes place through a power-based negotiation process involving private actors, but also local policymakers, authorities as well as intermediary agencies such as clubs, associations and NGOs. They act within a legal framework and with clear rules (i.e., construction law), following practices that are established in society.

Structures that result from a spacing in virtual space are much less regulated and, due to their abstract nature, are not much discussed by society. Companies have been making use of this freedom and established structures in cyberspace that the general public mostly uses or "fills up" with information instead of changing it. There is an imbalance of power between provider and user, which is expressed in a structural embedding of data collection capacity. Many digital applications require users to reveal personal information, and with every action they take in cyberspace, their transparency is increased. The new digital technologies record personal data, they exploit, analyse and store them. They do this across spaces, as they combine online and offline data, making use of the increasing options of data collection in (digitalised) real space as well. On data markets, data traders collect all the information and process it to meet the demand. The economic value of information on the user is expressed in numerous commercial exploitation contexts. For companies offering products and services, the dream of customer and market transparency seems to be coming true. They know about people's wishes, preferences, weaknesses, risks and needs, and they have the ability to take these into consideration immediately and exploit them commercially. This translation results in a data utilisation that reaches customers in a recursive manner by mirroring the familiar and keeping from them other content or information that could be instructive. By reflecting collected dispositions, it solidifies social classes. Ultimately, it confines individuals to their fully recorded biography, whereas personal development would result from breaking out of this biography. In this manner, the market directly intervenes in socialisation. In contrast to the goals of education policy, private actors aim at profit maximisation. The perpetuation of social conditions is not intended, but it is directly created through the practice of data utilisation.

The user is addressed recursively in four different ways. First of all, (Fig. 6.1a) personal data have an influence on cyberspace itself. Via ads, customer portals, social networks and news providers, what is shown and when can be determined in a personalised way. Invisible, externally defined algorithms decide over what is visible and what remains hidden, they offer incentives, draw boundaries and suggest what is suitable. The structures of the virtual sphere change in accordance with each user. Spacing in the virtual sphere is characterised by the ability to adapt specifically to each user. At the same time, offers and information reach the user directly (Fig. 6.1b) without a restrictive adaptation of the structures of virtual space. A tailored loan or the right insurance, offered via e-mail, for example, do not have an effect on the accessibility of cyberspace. However, they do represent offers that, due to their preselection, have a recursive effect. The numerous channels of personalised address, as exemplified in the empirical evaluation, again suggest a considerable influence on perception, on the definition of what is desirable and attainable. As digital forms of address are often based on characteristics of similarity of neighbourhood residents (cf. Chapter 5), they also have an indirect influence via the social environment.

In real space, the individual ability to perceive and act can also be distinguished in the two variants of direct data-based addressing on the one hand and data-based modification of the spatial structure on the other. As has been extensively demonstrated for the fields of marketing, people search or risk management and substantiated with further examples from the interconnected daily life, users are also targeted with more and more personalised offers and information offline. It must be assumed that sales talks and services (e.g., interactions in a store or at a hotel) will be making increasing use of existing information about customers. With the help of findings from business psychology, it is most likely that such interactions will be guided by economic, taste-related considerations.

Finally, the economic exploitation of personal data has an influence on the structure of real space. The increasing penetration of buildings and cities with interconnected objects (sentient city) creates further possibilities for addressing people with tailored content in their everyday lives (Fig. 6.1d). In the long run, it will not be necessary to use digital end devices such as smartphones, as cameras, sensors and auctors function independently. In such a spatial structure, in which virtual mirrors are embedded, the transitions to cyberspace become fluid.

While these developments can be dismissed as utopian, there are additional types of recursive acquisition regardless of the degree of interconnectedness. As clearly demonstrated by the empirical analysis of data trading, companies are already making use of digital databases to design spaces for specific target groups. As a consequence, the individual opportunity structure is highly dependent on which infrastructures, shops and product range are considered profitable in a neighbourhood. Exact data on the residents not only make it easy for companies and retailers to address them directly, but also to transfer their purchasing power and preferences into building structures and commercial products in real space. It is a spatial constitution by design where the arrangement of (urban) space can be organised in social correspondences. To the degree that people are addressed according to their milieu, socialisation influences become entrenched in a neighbourhood.

Therefore, the logic of social distinction and exclusion in a neighbourhood and of resource-dependent processes of arrangement need to be conceptualised differently in the age of digitalisation. It is a powerful spacing, accompanied by the economic valorisation of data (online as well as offline), which, together with the direct addressing of target groups, increasingly contributes to social stratification by a sorting of the socially suitable.

6.2 Outlook: Social Determination as an Overarching Challenge

In today's digitalised world, the old question of equality of opportunity and mobility in a society presents itself in a completely new form. The digital transformation is taking place at a time when social and sociospatial polarisation processes are being registered on a growing scale, as inequality is being discussed publicly against the backdrop of new job requirements, growing precariousness, rising revenues for real estate owners and dramatic rent increases (OECD 2019; Wacquant 2018; van Ham et al. 2021).

All these facts could give reason to assume that unequal opportunities for action will solidify and that spatial structures will persist which are characterised by limitations for the disadvantaged and benefits for the privileged. These are the conditions that the data-based economy finds itself under, and that it recursively takes up in numerous business fields, translating individual characteristics into suitable offers.

Cyberspace creates particularly favourable conditions for such a translation. For one thing, the data economy is able to use a medium the structures and conditions of which have not yet been questioned or influenced much by the users. What must never be forgotten is the fact that a large part of the offers of cyberspace are provided by private actors. In comparison with real space, large areas of the internet´s infrastructure are not financed by taxpayer money (as opposed to roads, public places or educational facilities), but have expanded thanks to private investors. The "road signs" relevant for orientation and "directions" (search engines) as well as the most popular sites of information exchange (social media sites) have a commercial orientation and function via personalised ads. The new digital sites of supply, information or entertainment in cyberspace are likewise oriented toward a valorisation of personal data. Correspondingly, the socialising influence of cyberspace must be interpreted primarily in the context of an economic logic of utilisation. Most of the content is aligned neither with social ideals like justice in general nor with concrete measures to foster inclusion, education and social mobility in particular. It is geared toward profit, the only guiding principle being the demand of its users, as opposed to set rules or goals of educational policy.

In the second place, the programmed spaces make it all but impossible for users to understand how the virtual offers directed at them are created. The interference into real space by powerful actors with a limiting effect on the individual becomes even more abstract with regard to cyberspace. The structures of cyberspace are based on programming causing a veiled form of spacing, and this is taking place under legal conditions that are still rather fuzzy or simply ineffective. These structures can permanently follow, protocol and contact the user, they can adapt individually and automatically, and they have a highly encouraging effect. Because of the individual use of cyberspace, users also miss out on the chance of a shared experience. This makes it more difficult to publicly discuss these structures on the basis of shared insights. As a result, in comparison with real space the opportunity to actively influence the conditions for action in the digital sphere diminishes.

Thirdly, by entering their data, users are confronted with a new form of remuneration for the use of the digital opportunity structure, the value of which they can hardly assess. Data processing is happening everywhere and at all times; it is becoming increasingly difficult to determine the origin and the goal of the data. As this data currency can benefit the most through recursive forms of address, it tends to personalise services, products and information in all areas of life. This targeting will become even more automatic with the growing use of artificial intelligence.

Many of these characteristics of cyberspace generally apply also to real space, which, from the point of view of private business, is constituted in a personalised way and which also evaluates, assesses and addresses. Even though economic interests are only partly involved, a rapidly growing ambient intelligence in cities or buildings is clearly emerging. In the complex interplay between cyberspace and digital real space, it is apparent that individuals are slowly being deprived of exclusive control over their privacy, while for businesses it is becoming easier to exploit personal preferences, online as well as offline.

As a consequence, a new conservative element is spreading in society which strongly limits social permeability in the age of digitalisation. The disadvantaged require a great deal of knowledge and effort to counter the increasing predetermination of the scope of individual opportunity. The same is true for policymakers, whose past attempts to mitigate neighbourhood effects with educational and infrastructure measures were already not very effective. Now, they are faced with the filter bubbles of the data economy which create social divides in cyberspace as well as in real space.

A preliminary assessment of the data revolution cannot overlook the fact that there are already numerous counter-movements that attempt to gain control over digital knowledge about the individual with the help of education, political action and protective measures. Successful initiatives like the European Directive on Data Protection notwithstanding, it is evident that the amount of personal data will only increase. So far, there is no indication that public awareness about the exploitation of data can keep up with the revolutionary technologies, the growing possibilities of data collection and the huge expansion of commercial business fields. Every day, new hardware and software solutions reach the market, offering price advantages, convenience, exclusive information and ubiquitous access to goods and services in real time—but in almost every case, consumers are required to reveal information about themselves.

On the other hand, simply abstaining from digital offers does not seem to make much sense. Given established communication practices, it would lead to self-isolation, entailing significant cost and information disadvantages. In our digitalised world, it is hardly possible to conceal individual characteristics anyway. Commercial providers will collect data about every individual, even those who try to reveal as few data as possible.

If they care about equal opportunity, policymakers must face the consolidation of social conditions due to the data economy and how it will shape the future. Laws for data protection will not be enough to keep up the promise of social mobility. Ultimately, the process of mirroring is about nothing less than economic actors displacing public institutions from spaces of socialisation.

As long as individual and institutionalised protection is not sufficiently effective, those affected could in the end be left with an adaptation strategy that, while bowing to the logic of segmentation, evaluation and allocation, specifically influences them. In order to escape the shackles of individual and milieu-related categorisation, databases would have to be provided with cross-milieu information, and a wide range of interests as well contradictions would have to be communicated. The opportunity to obtain these resources lies in the targeted disclosure of those attributes that are transformed into resources relevant to advancement. The implementation of this strategy would require a lot: In addition to the competence to leave habitualised dispositions behind, at least partially, in the display of interests and tastes (second digital divide), the ability to reflect on the technical and economic utilisation of data would be necessary. This would require an awareness that can only come about through education as well as a new understanding of the social system shaped by the data economy that is based on academic research. If this field of research benefits from a spatial perspective, as has been emphasised throughout this study, then spatial disciplines like geography can most certainly contribute more to this field.

The relationship between digitalisation and education is already part of the public discourse. In the future, labour markets will require more digital skills, and digitalisation also opens up new sources for individual education. Technological change is recognised to have the potential for professional and social mobilisation. However, an emphasis on the opportunities of empowerment clouds the fact that the digital transformation is also massively changing the spatial environment that conditions action. Without a critical look at the exploitation practice of the data economy in its social consequences, the opportunities for advancement in the age of digitalisation cannot be adequately grasped. Without a thorough exploration of the effectiveness of new spatial restrictions, the presorting of what is accessible cannot be understood. The promise of empowerment through digitisation is tied to conditions that place a heavy burden of responsibility on individuals, educational institutions, policymakers and, not least, academia. Thus, the message of the introductory slogan must also be understood as an urgent task: Where do you want to go today?

Bibliography

Betancourt, Michael (2016): *The critique of Digital Capitalism: An Analysis of the Political Economy of Digital Culture and Technology*. New York: Punctum Books.
Han, Byung-Chul (2013): *Transparenzgesellschaft*. Berlin: Matthes & Seitz.
Kropf, Jonathan & Laser, Stefan J. (eds.) (2019): *Digitale Bewertungspraktiken. Für eine Bewertungssoziologie des Digitalen*. Wiesbaden: Springer VS.
Lamont, Michèle; Beljean, Stefan & Chong, Phillippa (2015): *A Post-Bourdieusian Sociology of Valuation and Evaluation for the Field of Cultural Production*. New York: Routledge, 38–48.
Löw, Martina (2016): *The Sociology of Space: Materiality, Social Structures, and Action*. New York: Palgrave Macmillan.
Lupton, Deborah (2016): *The Quantified Self: A Sociology of Self-tracking*. Cambridge:Polity.
OECD (2019): OECD Employment Outlook 2019. Paris: OECD Publishing.
Van Ham, Maarten; Tammaru, Tiit; Ubarevičienė, Rūta & Janssen, Heleen (eds.) (2021): *Urban Socio-Economic Segregation and Income Inequality. A Global Perspective*. Cham: Springer.
Wacquant, Loïc (2018): *Die Verdammten der Stadt.—Eine vergleichende Soziologie fortgeschrittener Marginalität*. Wiesbaden: Springer VS.
Zuboff, Shoshana (2015): Big Other: Surveillance Capitalism and the Prospects of an Information Civilion. *Journal of Information Technology* 30, 75–89.

Open Access This chapter is licensed under the terms of the Creative Commons Attribution 4.0 International License (http://creativecommons.org/licenses/by/4.0/), which permits use, sharing, adaptation, distribution and reproduction in any medium or format, as long as you give appropriate credit to the original author(s) and the source, provide a link to the Creative Commons license and indicate if changes were made.

The images or other third party material in this chapter are included in the chapter's Creative Commons license, unless indicated otherwise in a credit line to the material. If material is not included in the chapter's Creative Commons license and your intended use is not permitted by statutory regulation or exceeds the permitted use, you will need to obtain permission directly from the copyright holder.

Bibliography

Aaltonen, Aleksi & Tempini, Niccoló (2014): Everything Counts in Large Amounts: A Critical Realist Case Study on Data-based Production. *Journal of Information Technology* 29 (1), 97–110.
Acquisti, Alessandro (2004): Privacy in Electronic Commerce and the Economics of Immediate Gratification. In: *Proceedings of the 5th ACM conference on Electronic commerce*, S. 21–29. Online: https://dl.acm.org/doi/10.1145/988772.988777 (01.03.2023)
Acquisti, Alessandro; John, Leslie K. & Loewenstein, George (2013): What Is Privacy Worth? In: The Journal of Legal Studies 42 (2), 249–274.
Ainsworth, James W. (2002): Why Does It Take a Village? The Mediation of Neighborhood Effects on Educational Achievement. *Social Forces* 81, 117–152.
Airoldi, Massimo (2022): *Machine Habitus: Toward a Sociology of Algorithms*. Cambridge: Polity.
Altrock, Uwe & Kunze, Ronald (Hrsg.) (2017): *Stadterneuerung und Armut. Jahrbuch Stadterneuerung 2016*. Wiesbaden: Springer VS.
Amoore, Louise & Piotukh, Volha (eds.) (2016): *Algorithmic Life: Calculative Devices in the Age of Big Data*. London, New York: Routledge.
Atkinson, Anthony B.; Piketty, Thomas & Saez, Emmanuel (2011): Top Incomes in the Long Run of History. *Journal of Economic Literature* 49 (1), 3–71.
Autor, David; Katz, Lawrence F. & Krueger, Alan B. (1999): Computing Inequality: Have Computers Changed the Labor Market? *Quarterly Journal of Economics* 113 (4), 1169–1214.
Bakshy, Eytan; Messing, Solomon & Adamic, Lada A. (2015): Political Science. Exposure to Ideologically Diverse News and Opinion on Facebook. *Science* 348 (6239), 1130–1132.

Bär, Paul Klaus-Dieter (2008): *Architekturpsychologie. Psychosoziale Aspekte des Wohnens.* Gießen: Psychosozial-Verlag.
Barberá, Pablo; Jost, John T.; Nagler, Jonathan; Tucker, Joshua A. & Bonneau, Richard (2015): Tweeting From Left to Right: Is Online Political Communication More Than an Echo Chamber? *Psychological Science* 26 (10), 1531–1542.
Bauman, Zygmunt & Lyon, David (2013): *Daten, Drohnen, Disziplin. Ein Gespräch über flüchtige Überwachung.* Berlin: Suhrkamp.
Bennett, Tony; Savage, Mike; Silva, Elizabeth; Warde, Alan; Gayo-Cal, Modesto & Wright, David (2009): *Culture, Class, Distinction.* New York: Routledge.
Benson, Michaela; Bridge, Gary & Wilson, Deborah (2015): School Choice in London and Paris—A Comparison of Middle-Class Strategies. *Social Policy & Administration* 49 (1), 24–43.
Berger, Joseph; Ridgeway, Cecilia, L. & Zelditch, Morris (2002): Construction of Status and Referential Structures. *Sociological Theory* 20 (2), 157–179.
Betancourt, Michael (2016): *The critique of Digital Capitalism: An Analysis of the Political Economy of Digital Culture and Technology.* New York: Punctum Books.
Beyvers, Eva; Helm, Paula; Hennig, Martin; Keckeis, Carmen; Innokentij, Kreknin & Püschel, Florian (eds.) (2017): *Räume und Kulturen des Privaten.* Wiesbaden: Springer VS.
Biermann, Ralf (2009): Die Bedeutung des Habitus-Konzepts für die Erforschung soziokultureller Unterschiede im Bereich der Medienpädagogik. *MedienPädagogik* 17, 1–18.
Blasius, Jörg; Friedrichs, Jürgen & Klöckner, Jennifer (2008): *Doppelt benachteiligt? Leben in einem deutsch-türkischen Stadtteil.* Wiesbaden: Springer VS.
Blattberg, Robert C.; Kim, Byung-Do & Neslin, Scott A. (2008): *Database marketing. Analyzing and managing customers.* New York: Springer.
Bohn, Angela; Buchta, Christian; Hornik, Kurt & Mair, Patrick (2014): Making Friends and Communicating on Facebook: Implications for the Access to Social Capital. *Social Networks* 37, 29–41.
Bound, John & Johnson, George (1992): Changes in the Structure of Wages in the 1980s: An Evaluation of Alternative Explanations. *American Economic Review* 83, 371–392.
Bourdieu, Pierre (1979): *Entwurf einer Theorie der Praxis auf der ethnologischen Grundlage der Kabylischen Gesellschaft.* Frankfurt a. M.: Suhrkamp.
Bourdieu, Pierre (1983): Ökonomisches Kapital, kulturelles Kapital, soziales Kapital. In: Reinhard Kreckel (Hrsg.): Soziale Ungleichheiten. Göttingen: Schwartz, S. 183–198.

Bourdieu, Pierre (1984): *Distinction. A Social Critique of the Judgement of Taste*. New York, London: Routledge.
Bourdieu, Pierre (1991): Physischer, sozialer und angeeigneter physischer Raum. In: Martin Wentz (Hrsg.): *Stadt-Räume*. Frankfurt a. M.: Campus Verlag, 25–34.
Bourdieu, Pierre (1999): *The Weight of the World: Social Suffering in Contemporary Society*. Stanford, CA.: Stanford University Press.
Bourdieu, Pierre & Wacquant, Loïc (2013): *Reflexive Anthropologie*. Frankfurt a. M.: Suhrkamp.
Boutyline, Andrei & Willer, Robb (2017): The Social Structure of Political Echo Chambers: Variation in Ideological Homophily in Online Networks. *Political Psychology* 38 (3), 551–569.
Boyd, Danah (2014): *Es ist kompliziert. Das Leben der Teenager in sozialen Netzwerken*. München: Redline Verlag.
Bozdag, Engin & van den Hoven, Jeroen (2015): Breaking the Filter Bubble: Democracy and Design. *Ethics and Information Technology* 17 (4), 249–265.
Brüggen, Nils & Schemmerling, Mareike (2014): Das Social Web und die Aneignung von Sozialräumen. Forschungsperspektiven auf das sozialraumbezogene Medienhandeln von Jugendlichen in Sozialen Netzwerkdiensten. In: *sozialraum.de* 6 (1). Online: https://www.sozialraum.de/das-social-web-und-die-aneignung-von-sozialraeumen.php (01.03.2023)
Buhtz, Katharina; Reinartz, Annika; Koenig, Andreas; Graf-Vlachy, Lorenz & Mammen, Jan (2014): Second-Order Digital Inequality: The Case of E-Commerce. *International Conference on Information Systems*. Online: https://ssrn.com/abstract=2876126. (01.03.2023)
Bujlow, Tomasz; Carela-Español, Valentín; Solé-Pareta, Josep; & Barlet-Ros Pere (2017): A Survey on Web Tracking: Mechanisms, Implications, and Defenses. *Proceedings of the IEEE* 105 (8), 1476–1510.
Castel, Robert (2000): *Die Metamorphosen der sozialen Frage*. Konstanz: UVK Verlagsgesellschaft.
Castells, Manuel (2009): *The Rise of the Network Society*. Vol. 1. Hoboken: Wiley-Blackwell.
Chancel, Lucas; Piketty, Thomas; Saez, Emmanuel & Zucman, Gabriel (2022): *World Inequality Report 2022*. Cambridge: Harvard University Press.
Cheung, Anne S.Y. (2014): Location Privacy: The Challenges of Mobile Service Devices. *Computer Law & Security Review* 30 (1), 41–54.
Choudhury, Amitava; Biswas, Arindam & Chakraborti, Sadhan (eds.) (2023): *Digital Learning Based Education Transcending Physical Barriers*. Singapore: Springer Nature.
Cocchia, Annalisa (2014): Smart and Digital City: A Systematic Literature Review. In: Renata Paola Dameri & Camille Rosenthal-Sabroux (eds.): *Smart*

City. How to Create Public and Economic Value with High Technology in Urban Space. Cham: Springer, 13–43.

Colleoni, Elanor; Rozza, Alessandro & Arvidsson, Adam (2014): Echo Chamber or Public Sphere? Predicting Political Orientation and Measuring Political Homophily in Twitter Using Big Data. *Journal of Communication* 64 (2), 317–332.

Crang, Michel & Graham, Stephen (2007): Sentient Cities: Ambient Intelligence and the Politics of Urban Space. *Information, Communication & Society* 10 (6), 789–817.

Cucca, Roberta & Ranci, Costanzo (2017): *Unequal Cities: The Challenge of Post-Industrial Transition in Times of Austerity*. London: Routledge.

Cuijpers, Colette & Koops, Bert-Jaap (2013): Smart Metering and Privacy in Europe: Lessons from the Dutch Case. In: Serge Gutwirth, Ronald Leenes, Paul de Hert & Yves Poullet (eds.): *European Data Protection: Coming of Age*. Dordrecht: Springer Netherlands, 269–293.

Cushion, Christopher J. & Jones, Robyn L. (2012): A Bourdieusian Analysis of Cultural Reproduction: Socialisation and the 'Hidden Curriculum' in Professional Football. *Sport, Education and Society* 19 (3), 276–298.

Dameri, Renata Paola & Rosenthal-Sabroux, Camille (eds.) (2014): *Smart City. How to Create Public and Economic Value with High Technology in Urban Space*. Cham: Springer.

Dangschat, Jens S. (2017): Armut und Stadterneuerung—zwei Seiten einer Medallie? In: Uwe Altrock & Ronald Kunze (eds.): *Stadterneuerung und Armut. Jahrbuch Stadterneuerung 2016*. Wiesbaden: Springer VS, 13–35.

Daniela, Linda (ed.) (2022): *Inclusive Digital Education*. Cham: Springer.

De Maio, Fernando G. & Benjamins, Maureen R. (eds.) (2021): *Unequal Cities: Structural Racism and the Death Gap in America's 30 Largest Cities*. Baltimore: Johns Hopkins University Press.

Deffner, Veronika & Haferburg, Christoph. (2012): Raum, Stadt und Machtverhältnisse. Humangeographische Auseinandersetzungen mit Bourdieu. *Geographische Zeitschrift* 100 (3), 164–180.

Deutsche Bundesbank (2022): Eine verteilungsbasierte Vermögensbilanz der privaten Haushalte in Deutschland—Ergebnisse und Anwendungen. Monatsbericht Juni 2022. Online: https://www.bundesbank.de/resource/blob/894880/958edb67dec48f1dbdeccaf0efd36768/mL/2022-07-vermoegensbilanz-data.pdf (01.03.2023)

Deutsches Institut für Vertrauen und Sicherheit im Internet (DIVSI) (2016): DIVSI Internet-Milieus 2016. Die digitalisierte Gesellschaft in Bewegung. Hamburg. Online: https://www.divsi.de/publikationen/studien/divsi-internet-milieus-2016-die-digitalisierte-gesellschaft-bewegung/index.html (01.03.2023)

Dimaggio, Paul. (1979). On Pierre Bourdieu. Review essay on Outline of a Theory of Practice by Pierre Bourdieu and Reproduction: In Education, Society and Culture by Pierre Bourdieu and Jean-Claude Passeron. *American Journal of Sociology* 84 (6).

DiMaggio, Paul; Hargittai, Eszter; Neuman, Russell W. & Robinson, John P. (2001): Social Implications of the Internet. *Annual. Review of Sociology* 27, S307–336.

Döring, Lisa (2015): Biografieeffekte und intergenerationale Sozialisationseffekte in Mobilitätsbiografien. In: Joachim Scheiner & Christian Holz-Rau (eds.): *Räumliche Mobilität und Lebenslauf*. Wiesbaden: Springer VS, 23–41.

Droste, Friedrich (2014): *Die strategische Manipulation der elektronischen Mundpropaganda. Eine spieltheoretische Analyse*. Wiesbaden: Springer Gabler.

Druyen, Thomas C. J.; Lauterbach, Wolfgang & Grundmann, Matthias (eds.) (2009): *Reichtum und Vermögen. Zur gesellschaftlichen Bedeutung von Reichtums- und Vermögensforschung*. Wiesbaden: Springer VS.

Dwyer, Catherine (2009): Behavioral Targeting: A Case Study of Consumer Tracking on Levis.com. *Proceedings of the Fifteenth Americas Conference on Information Systems*, 1–10.

Dylko, Ivan; Dolgov, Igor; Hoffman, William; Eckhart, Nicholas; Molina, Maria & Aaziz, Omar (2017): The Dark Side of Technology: An Experimental Investigation of the Influence of Customizability Technology on Online Political Selective Exposure. *Computers in Human Behavior* 73, 181–190.

Ecarius, Jutta; Köbel, Nils & Wahl, Katrin (2011): *Familie, Erziehung und Sozialisation*. Wiesbaden: Springer VS.

Ellison, Nicole B.; Steinfield, Charles & Lampe, Cliff (2007): The Benefits of Facebook 'Friends': Exploring the Relationship Between College Students' Use of Online Social Networks and Social Capital. *Journal of Computer-mediated Communication* 12, 1143–1168.

Ellison, Nicole B.; Steinfield, Charles & Lampe, Cliff (2011): Connection Strategies: Social Capital Implications of Facebook-enabled Communication Practices. *New Media & Society* 13 (6), 873–892.

Eubanks, Virginia (2018): *Automating Inequality. How High-Tech Tools Profile, Police and Punish the Poor*. New York: St Martin's Press.

Federal Trade Commission (2014): *Data Brokers. A Call for Transparency and Accountability*. Washington.

Felser, Georg (2015): *Werbe- und Konsumentenpsychologie*. Berlin, Heidelberg: Springer-Verlag Berlin Heidelberg.

Ferger, Edwin (2018): Anwendungen der Informations- und Kommunikationstechnologie und die Mediatisierung sozialer Inklusion. In: Aljoscha Burchardt & Hans Uszkoreit (eds.): *IT für soziale Inklusion*. Berlin, Boston: De Gruyter, 69–76.

Florida, Richard; Adler, Patrick & Mellander, Charlotta (2017): The City as Innovation Machine. *Regional Studies* 51 (1), 86–96.
Foucault, Michel (1979): *Discipline and Punish: The Birth of the Prison.* Alexandria: Alexander Street Press.
Frick, Joachim R. & Grabka, Markus M. (2009): Zur Entwicklung der Vermögensungleichheit in Deutschland. *Berlin Journal für Soziologie* 19 (4), 577–600.
Gabrys, Jennifer (2014): Programming Environments: Environmentality and Citizen Sensing in the Smart City. *Environment and Planning D* 32 (1), 30–48.
Giddens, Anthony (1984): *The Constitution of Society. Outline of the Theory of Structuration.* Cambridge: Polity Press.
Glăveanu, Vlad; Ness, Ingunn & Saint Laurent, Constance de (eds.) (2020): *Creative Learning in Digital and Virtual Environments. Opportunities and Challenges of Technology-Enabled Learning and Creativity.* New York: Routledge.
Goldhammer, Klaus & Wiegand, André (2017): Ökonomischer Wert von Verbraucherdaten für Adress- und Datenhändler. Goldmedia GmbH Strategy Consulting. Berlin. Online: https://www.bmj.de/SharedDocs/Downloads/DE/PDF/Berichte/Oekon_Wert_Daten_Adresshaendler.pdf?__blob=publicationFile (01.03.2023)
Gong, Huiwen; Hassink, Robert & Maus, Gunnar (2017): What does Pokémon Go teach us about geography? *Geographica Helvetica* 72 (2), 227–230.
Gornig, Martin & Goebel, Jan (2013): Ökonomischer Strukturwandel und Polarisierungstendenzen in deutschen Stadtregionen. In: Martin Kronauer & Walter Siebel (Hrsg.): *Polarisierte Städte. Soziale Ungleichheit als Herausforderung für die Stadtpolitik.* Frankfurt a. M.: Campus Verlag, S. 51–68.
Grabbert, Tammo (2008): *Schrumpfende Städte und Segregation. Eine vergleichende Studie über Leipzig und Essen.* Berlin: Wissenschaftlicher Verlag.
Graham, Mark & Anwar, Mohammad Amir (2019): Labour. In: James Ash, Rob Kitchin & Agnieszka Leszczynski (eds.): *Digital Geographies.* Los Angeles: Sage, 177–187.
Greenspan, Anna (2021): QR Codes and the Sentient City. *Studia Neophilologica* 93 (2), 206–218.
Haandrikman, Karen; Costa, Rafael; Malmberg, Bo; Rogne, Adrian Farner; Sleutjes, Bart (2023): Socio-economic Segregation in European Cities. A Comparative Study of Brussels, Copenhagen, Amsterdam, Oslo and Stockholm. *Urban Geography* 44 (1), 1–36.
Hahn, Kornelia (2021): *Social Digitalisation: Persistent Transformations Beyond Digital Technology.* Cham: Palgrave Macmillan.
Han, Byung-Chul (2013): Transparenzgesellschaft. Berlin: Matthes & Seitz.

Hargittai, Eszter & Hinnant, Amanda (2008): Digital Inequality. *Communication Research* 35 (5), 602–621.

Harvey, David (2008): The Right to the City. *New Left Review* 53, 23–40.

Hatlevik, Ove Edvard & Christophersen, Knut-Andreas (2013): Digital Competence at the Beginning of Upper Secondary School: Identifying Factors Explaining Digital Inclusion. *Computers & Education* 63, 240–247.

Häußermann, Hartmut & Siebel, Walter (2004): *Stadtsoziologie. Eine Einführung*. Frankfurt a. M.: Campus Verlag.

Helbig, Marcel & Jähnen, Stefanie (2018): Wie brüchig ist die soziale Architektur unserer Städte? Trends und Analysen der Segregation in 74 deutschen Städten. Wissenschaftszentrum Berlin für Sozialforschung GmbH. Berlin. Online: https://www.econstor.eu/handle/10419/179001 (01.03.2023)

Hellbrück, Jürgen & Fischer, Manfred (1999): *Umweltpsychologie. Ein Lehrbuch*. Göttingen: Hogrefe Verlag.

Henderson, Marlone D.; Wakslak, Cheryl J.; Fujita, Kentaro & Rohrbach, John (2011): Construal Level Theory and Spatial Distance. *Social Psychology* 42 (3), 165–173.

Herland, Matthew; Khoshgoftaar, Taghi M. & Wald, Randall (2014): A Review of Data Mining Using Big Data in Health Informatics. *Journal of Big Data* 1 (2), 1–35.

Herrmann, Heike (2010): Raumbegriffe und Forschungen zum Raum—eine Einleitung. In: Heike Herrmann (ed.): *RaumErleben. Zur Wahrnehmung des Raumes in Wissenschaft und Praxis*. Opladen: Budrich, 7–30.

Hilbert, Martin & López, Priscila (2011): The World's Technological Capacity to Store, Communicate, and Compute Information. *Science* 332 (6025), 60–65.

Hirsh, Jacob B.; Kang, Sonia K. & Bodenhausen, Galen V. (2012): Personalized Persuasion: Tailoring Persuasive Appeals to Recipients' Personality Traits. *Psychological Science* 23 (6), 578–581.

Holm, Andrej (2011): Kosten der Unterkunft als Segregationsmotor. Befunde aus Berlin und Oldenburg. *Informationen zur Raumentwicklung* (9), 557–566.

Holm, Andrej (2016): Gentrification und das Ende der Berliner Mischung. In: Eberhard von Einem (ed.): *Wohnen*. Wiesbaden: Springer, 191–231.

Holm, Andrej & Gebhardt, Dirk (2011): *Initiativen für ein Recht auf Stadt. Theorie und Praxis städtischer Aneignung*. Hamburg: VSA-Verlag.

Holt, Douglas B. (1997): Distinction in America? Recovering Bourdieu's Theory of Tastes from its Critics. *Poetics* 25, 93–120.

Holz-Rau, Christian & Scheiner, Joachim (2015): Mobilitätsbiografien und Mobilitätssozialisation: Neue Zugänge zu einem alten Thema. In: Joachim Scheiner & Christian Holz-Rau (eds.): *Räumliche Mobilität und Lebenslauf*. Wiesbaden: Springer VS, 3–22.

Hotho, Andreas; Pedersen, Rasmus Ulslev & Wurst, Michael (2010): Ubiquitous Data. In: Michael May & Lorenza Saitta (eds.): *Ubiquitous Knowledge Discovery*. Berlin, Heidelberg: Springer, 61–74.
Housley, William; Edwards, Adam; Beneito-Montagut, Roser & Fitzgerald, Richard (eds.) (2022): *The SAGE Handbook of Digital Society*. Los Angeles, London, New Delhi: Sage.
Hradil, Stefan (2001): *Soziale Ungleichheit in Deutschland*. Wiesbaden: Springer VS.
Hurrelmann, Klaus & Bauer, Ullrich (2018): *Socialisation During the Life Course*. New York, London: Routledge.
Iske, Stefan; Klein, Alex; Kutscher, Nadia & Otto, Hans-Uwe (2007): Virtuelle Ungleichheit und informelle Bildung: eine empirische Analyse der Internnutzung Jugendlicher und ihre Bedeutung für Bildung und gesellschaftliche Teilhabe. In: Hans-Uwe Otto (ed.): *Grenzenlose Cyberwelt? Zum Verhältnis von digitaler Ungleichheit und neuen Bildungszugängen für Jugendliche*. Wiesbaden: Springer VS, 65–92.
Iske, Stefan; Klein, Alexandra & Kutscher, Nadia (2005): Differences in Internet Usage—Social Inequality and Informal Education. *Social Work & Society* 3 (2), 215–223.
Jacobson, Susan; Myung, Eunyoung & Johnson, Steven L. (2016): Open Media or Echo Chamber: The Use of Links in Audience Discussions on the Facebook Pages of Partisan News Organizations. *Information, Communication & Society* 19 (7), 875–891.
Jin, Haojian; Yang, Zhijian; Kumar, Swarun & Hong, Jason (2018): Towards Wearable Everyday Body-Frame Tracking using Passive RFIDs. *Proceedings of ACM on Interactive, Mobile, Wearable and Ubiquitous Technologies* 1 (4), 1–23.
Kakwani, Nanak (2022): *Economic Inequality and Poverty Facts, Methods, and Policies*. Oxford: Oxford University Press.
Kammer, Matthias (2014): *Kinder, Jugendliche und junge Erwachsene in der digitalen Welt. Eine Grundlagenstudie des SINUS-Instituts Heidelberg und des Deutschen Instituts für Vertrauen und Sicherheit im Internet* (DIVSI). Hamburg.
Khoury, Muin J. & Ioannidis, John (2014): Medicine. Big Data Meets Public Health. *Science* 346 (6213), 1054–1055.
King, Anthony (2000): Thinking with Bourdieu Against Bourdieu: A "Practical" Critique of the Habitus. *Sociological Theory* 18 (3), 417–433.
Kitchin, Rob & Dodge, Martin (2011): *Code/Space: Software and Everyday Life*. Cambridge: MIT Press.
Klauser, Francisco; Paasche, Till & Söderström, Ola (2014): Michel Foucault and the Smart City: Power Dynamics Inherent in Contemporary Governing Through Code. *Environment and Planning. D* 32 (5), 869–885.

Koput, Kenneth (2010): *Social Capital an Introduction to Managing Networks*. Northampton, Mass, Edward Elgar.
Krajewski, Christian (2015): Arm, sexy und immer teurer. *Standort* 39 (2-3), 77–85.
Kreckel, Reinhard (1992): *Politische Soziologie der sozialen Ungleichheit*. Frankfurt a. M.: Campus Verlag.
Kreutzer, Ralf & Land, Karl-Heinz (2015): *Digital Darwinism. Branding and Business Models in Jeopardy*. Berlin, Heidelberg: Springer.
Kronauer, Martin & Siebel, Walter (eds.) (2013): *Polarisierte Städte. Soziale Ungleichheit als Herausforderung für die Stadtpolitik*. Frankfurt a. M.: Campus Verlag.
Kronauer, Martin & Vogel, Martin (2004): Erfahrung und Bewältigung von sozialer Ausgrenzung in der Großstadt: Was sind Quartierseffekte, was Lageeffekte? In: Hartmut Häußermann, Martin Kronauer & Walter Siebel (eds.): *An den Rändern der Städte. Armut und Ausgrenzung*. Frankfurt a. M.: Suhrkamp, 235–257.
Kropf, Jonathan & Laser, Stefan J. (eds.) (2019): *Digitale Bewertungspraktiken. Für eine Bewertungssoziologie des Digitalen*. Wiesbaden: Springer VS.
Lambert, Alex (2016): Intimacy and Social Capital on Facebook: Beyond the Psychological Perspective. *New Media & Society* 18 (11), 2559–2575.
Lamont, Michèle; Beljean, Stefan & Chong, Phillippa (2015): *A Post-Bourdieusian Sociology of Valuation and Evaluation for the Field of Cultural Production*. New York: Routledge, 38–48.
Lampert, Thomas & Rosenbrock, Rolf (2017): Armut und Gesundheit. In: Der Paritätische Gesamtverband (eds.): *Bericht zur Armutsentwicklung in Deutschland 2017*. Berlin, 98–108.
Lauen, Lee (2016): Contextual Explanations of School Choice. *Sociology of Education* 80 (3), 179–209.
Levy, Frank & Murnane, Richard J. (1992): U.S. Earnings and Earnings Inequality: A Review of Recent Trends and Proposed Explanations. *Journal of Economic Literature* 30, 1333–1381.
Löw, Martina (2016): *The Sociology of Space: Materiality, Social Structures, and Action*. New York: Palgrave Macmillan.
Lupton, Deborah (2016): *The Quantified Self: A Sociology of Self-tracking*. Cambridge:Polity.
Lyon, David (Hrsg.) (2003): *Surveillance as Social Sorting: Privacy, Risk, and Digital Discrimination*. London, New York: Routledge.
Lyon, David (2018): *The Culture of Surveillance*. Cambridge: Polity.
Mackert, Jürgen (ed.) (2004): *Die Theorie sozialer Schließung. Tradition, Analysen, Perspektiven*. Wiesbaden: Springer VS.
Manago, Adriana M.; Taylor, Tamara & Greenfield, Patricia M. (2012): Me and my 400 friends: The Anatomy of College Students' Facebook Networks, their

Communication Patterns, and well-being. *Developmental psychology* 48 (2), 369–380.
Martens, Rudolf (2011): Armutsberichterstattung und Regelsatzanpassung für Ballungsräume: das Beispiel München. In: Bernd Belina, Norbert Gestring, Wolfgang Müller & Detlev Sträter (eds.): *Urbane Differenzen. Disparitäten innerhalb und zwischen Städten*. Münster: Westfälisches Dampfboot, 163–183.
Meyen, Michael (2007): Medienwissen und Medienmenüs als kulturelles Kapital und als Distinktionsmerkmale. Eine Typologie der Mediennutzer in Deutschland. *Medien & Kommunikationswissenschaft* 55 (3), 333–354.
Michael, Katina & Clarke, Roger (2013): Location and Tracking of Mobile Devices: Überveillance Stalks the Streets. *Computer Law & Security Review* 29 (3), 216–228.
Michael, Katina & Michael, M. G. (2011): The Social and Behavioural Implications Of Location-based Services. *Journal of Location Based Services* 5 (3-4), 121–137.
Miethe, Ingrid; Tervooren, Anja & Ricken, Norbert (eds.) (2017): *Bildung und Teilhabe*. Wiesbaden: Springer VS.
Millonig, Alexandra & Gartner, Georg (2011): Identifying Motion and Interest Patters of Shoppers for Developing Personalized Wayfinding Tools. *Journal of Location Based Services* 3 (1), 3–21.
Mitchell, William J. (1996): *City of Bits. Space, Place, and the Infobahn*. Cambridge: MIT Press.
MPFS (ed.) (2019): JIM-Studie 2019. Jugend. Information. Medien. Stuttgart. Online: https://www.mpfs.de/fileadmin/files/Studien/JIM/2019/JIM_2019.pdf (01.03.2023)
Musterd, Sako; Tammaru, Tiit; Marcinczak, Szymon & van Ham, Maarten (eds.) (2015): *Socio-Economic Segregation in European Capital Cities: East Meets West*. Milton Park: Taylor and Francis.
Musterd, Sako; Marcińczak, Szymon; van Ham, Maarten and Tammaru, Tiit (2017): Socioeconomic Segregation in European Capital Cities. Increasing Separation Between Poor and Rich. *Urban Geography* 38 (7), 1062–1083.
Negroponte, Nicolas (1995): *Total Digital—Die Welt zwischen 0 und 1 oder: Die Zukunft der Kommunikation*. München: Goldmann.
OECD (2018): Divided Cities. *Understanding Intra-urban Inequalities*. Paris: OECD Publishing.
OECD (2019): OECD Employment Outlook 2019. Paris: OECD Publishing.
O' Mahony, Stephen (2015): A Proposed Model for the Approach to Augmented Reality Deployment in Marketing Communications. *Procedia—Social and Behavioral Sciences* (175), 227–235. Online: https://isiarticles.com/bundles/Article/pre/pdf/41113.pdf (01.03.2023)
Otto, Hans-Uwe; Kutscher, Nadia; Klein, Alexandra & Iske, Stefan (2005): *Soziale Ungleichheit im virtuellen Raum: Wie nutzen Jugendliche das*

Internet? Erste Ergebnisse einer empirischen Untersuchung zu Online-Nutzungsdifferenzen und Aneignungsstrukturen von Jugendlichen. Berlin.
Pariser, Eli (2011): *Filter Bubble. What the Internet is Hiding from you.* New York: The Penguin Press.
Partzsch, Dieter (1970): *Handwörterbuch der Raumforschung + Raumordnung.* Hannover: Jänecke.
Plate, Elke; Polinna, Cordelia & Tonndorf, Thorsten (2014): Aufwertung. Verdrängung. Soziale Mischung sichern. Das Beispiel Berlin. *Informationen zur Raumentwicklung* (4), 291–304.
Pentland, Alex; Lipton, Alexander & Hardjono, Thomas (2021): *Building the New Economy: Data As Capital.* Cambridge, MIT Press.
Petmecky, Andrea (2008): *Architektur von Entwicklungsumwelten. Umweltaneignung und -wahrnehmung im Kindergarten.* Marburg: Tectum-Verlag.
Piketty, Thomas (2014): *Capital in the Twenty-First Century.* Cambridge: Harvard University Press.
Piketty, Thomas & Saez, Emmanuel (2006): The Evolution of Top Incomes: A Historical and International Perspective. *American Economic Review* 96 (2), 200–205.
Power, Daniel, J. (2015): Creating a Data-Driven Global Society. In: Iyer Lakshmi & Daniel, J. Power (eds.): *Reshaping Society through Analytics, Collaboration, and Decision Support. Role of Business Intelligence and Social Media.* Cham: Springer, 13–28.
Prieur, Annick; Rosenlund, Lennart & Skjott-Larsen, Jakob (2008): Cultural capital today. A case study from Denmark. *Poetics* 36, 45–71.
Quillian, Lincoln; Lagrange, Hugues (2016): Socioeconomic Segregation in Large Cities in France and the United States. *Demography* 53 (4), 1051–1084.
Ragnedda, Massimo (2017): *The Third Digital Divide. A Weberian Approach to Digital Inequalities.* New York: Routledge.
Ragnedda, Massimo & Ruiu, Maria Laura (2018): Social Capital and the Three Levels of Digital Divide. In: Ibid. & Glenn W. Muschert (eds.): *Theorizing Digital Divides.* Milton: Routledge, 21–34.
Renner, Karl-Heinz; Schütz, Astrid & Machilek, Franz (eds.) (2005): *Internet und Persönlichkeit. Differentiell-psychologische und diagnostische Aspekte der Internetnutzung.* Göttingen: Hogrefe Verlag.
Rheingold, Howard (1994): *Virtuelle Gemeinschaft: soziale Beziehungen im Zeitalter des Computers.* Boston: Addison-Wesley.
Ridgeway, Claudia (2014): Why Status Matters for Inequality. *American Sociological Review* 79 (1), 1–16.
Rienties, Bart C.; Hampel, Regine; Scanlon, Eileen & Whitelock, Denise (eds.) (2022): *Open World Learning: Research, Innovation and the Challenges of High-Quality Education.* London: Routledge.

Robinson, John P.; DiMaggio, Paul & Hargittai, Eszter (2003): New Social Survey Perspectives on the Digital Divide. *IT & Society* 1 (5), 1–22.
Rohlinger, Deana A. & Sobieraj, Sarah (2022): *The Oxford Handbook of Digital Media Sociology*. New York: Oxford University Press.
Rohrbach, Daniela (2008): *Wissensgesellschaft und soziale Ungleichheit. Ein Zeit- und Ländervergleich*. Wiesbaden: Springer VS.
Rössel, Jörg (2009): *Sozialstrukturanalyse. Eine kompakte Einführung*. Wiesbaden: Springer VS.
Rutten, Roel; Westlund, Hans & Boekema, Frans (2010): The Spatial Dimension of Social Capital. *European Planning Studies* 18 (6), 863–871.
Safransky, Sara (2020): Geographies of Algorithmic Violence: Redlining the Smart City. *International Journal of Urban and Regional Research* 44 (2), 200–218.
Sassen, Saskia (1994): *Cities in a World Economy. Sociology for a New Century*. Thousand Oaks, London, New Dehli: SAGE Publications.
Sassen, Saskia (2001): *The Global City*. New York, London, Tokyo. Princeton: Princeton University Press.
Schauster, Erin. E.; Ferrucci, Patrick & Neill, Marlene S. (2016): Native Advertising Is the New Journalism: How Deception Affects Social Responsibility. *American Behavioral Scientist* (6), 1–17.
Scheffer, Jörg & Voss, Martin (2008): Die Privatisierung der Sozialisation—Der Soziale Raum als heimlicher Lehrplan im Wandel. In: Petia Genkova (ed.): *Erfolg durch Schlüsselqualifikationen? "heimliche Lehrpläne" und Basiskompetenzen im Zeichen der Globalisierung*. Lengerich: Pabst Science Publishers, 102–115.
Schmidt, Ana Lucía; Zollo, Fabiana; Del Vicario, Michela; Bessi, Alessandro; Scala, Antonio; Caldarelli, Guido et al. (2017): Anatomy of news consumption on Facebook. *Proceedings of the National Academy of Sciences of the United States of America* 114 (12), 3035–3039.
Schmidt, Jan Hinrik; Paus-Hasebrink, Ingrid & Hasebrink, Uwe (eds.) (2009): *Heranwachsen mit dem Social Web. Zur Rolle von Web 2.0-Angeboten im Alltag von Jugendlichen und jungen Erwachsenen*. Berlin: Vistas-Verlag.
Schnur, Olaf (2013): Zwischen Stigma, Subvention und Selbstverantwortung. Ambivalenzen der Quartiersentwicklung in Berlin. *Geographische Rundschau* 65 (2), 28–36.
Schroer, Markus (2006): *Räume, Orte, Grenzen. Auf dem Weg zu einer Soziologie des Raums*. Frankfurt a. M.: Suhrkamp.
Schürz, Martin (2016): Die Rückkehr der sozialen Frage. *Zeitschrift für Individualpsychologie* 41 (3), 197–206.
Sheller, Mimi (2014): The New Mobilities Paradigm for a Live Sociology. *Current Sociology Review* 62 (6), 789–811.

Shepard, Marc (ed.) (2011): *Sentient City. Ubiquitous Computing, Architecture, and the Future of Urban Space*. Cambridge: MIT Press.
Stadt München (2017): Regionaler Sozialatlas München. Online: http://mstatistik-muenchen.de/regionalersozialatlas/2017/atlas.html.
Siebel, Walter (2012): Stadt und soziale Ungleichheit. *Leviathan* 40 (3), 462–475.
Spohr, Dominic (2017): Fake News and Ideological Polarization: Filter Bubbles and Selective Exposure on Social Media. *Business Information Review* 34 (3), 150–160.
Steinfield, Charles; Ellison, Nicole B. & Lampe, Cliff (2008): Social Capital, Self-esteem, and Use of Online Social Network Sites: A Longitudinal Analysis. *Journal of Applied Developmental Psychology* 29 (6), 434–445.
Strohmeier, Klaus Peter (2006): Segregation in den Städten. Bonn: Friedrich-Ebert-Stiftung Abt. Wirtschafts- und Sozialpolitik (Gesprächskreis Migration und Integration). Online: http://library.fes.de/pdf-files/asfo/04168.pdf. (01.03.2023)
Subrahmanyam, Kaveri; Reich, Stephanie M.; Waechter, Natalia & Espinoza, Guadalupe (2008): Online and Offline Social Networks: Use of Social Networking Sites by Emerging Adults. *Journal of Applied Developmental Psychology* 29 (6), 420–433.
Suler, John, R. (2015): *Psychology of the Digital Age. Humans become electric*. Cambridge: Cambridge University Press.
Thiedeke, Udo (ed.) (2004): *Soziologie des Cyberspace. Medien, Strukturen und Semantiken*. Wiesbaden: Springer VS.
Thrift, Nigel (2014): The 'Sentient' City and What It May Portend. *Big Data & Society* 1 (1), 1–21.
Turkle, Sherry (1998): *Leben im Netz. Identität in Zeiten des Internet*. Reinbek bei Hamburg: Rowohlt.
United Nations (2020): *World Social Report 2020. Inequality in a Rapidly Changing World*. Online: https://www.un.org/development/desa/dspd/wp-content/uploads/sites/22/2020/02/World-Social-Report2020-FullReport.pdf. (01.03.2023)
Urry, John (2007): *Mobilities*. Cambridge: Polity.
Valkenburg, Patti M. (2017): Understanding Self-Effects in Social Media. *Human Communication Research* 43 (4), 477–490.
Van Dijk, Jan A.G.M. (2014): The Evolution of the Digital Divide: The Digital Divide Turns to Inequality of Skills and Usage. *New Media & Society* 16 (3), S. 507–526.
Van Dijk, Jan A.G.M (2020): *The Digital Divide*. Cambridge: Polity Press.
Van Ham, Maarten; Tammaru, Tiit; Ubarevičienė, Rūta & Janssen, Heleen (eds.) (2021): *Urban Socio-Economic Segregation and Income Inequality. A Global Perspective*. Cham: Springer.

Wacquant, Loïc (2018): *Die Verdammten der Stadt.—Eine vergleichende Soziologie fortgeschrittener Marginalität*. Wiesbaden: Springer VS.
Wang, Dan; Park, Sangwon & Fesenmaier, Daniel R. (2012): The Role of Smartphones in Mediating the Touristic Experience. *Journal of Travel Research* 51 (4), 371–387.
Wang, Dan; Xiang, Zheng & Fesenmaier, Daniel R. (2016): Smartphone Use in Everyday Life and Travel. *Journal of Travel Research* 55 (1), 52–63.
Weiqin, Eliza Leong; Campbell, Marilyn; Kimpton, Melanie; Wozencroft, Kelly & Orel, Alexandra (2016): Social Capital on Facebook. *Journal of Educational Computing Research* 54 (6), 747–786.
Wetzstein, Steffen (2018): Bezahlbares städtisches Wohnen im internationalen Vergleich. *Informationen zur Raumentwicklung* (4), 34–47.
Wiewiorra, Lukas (2018): Transparenz und Kontrolle in der Datenökonomie. *Wirtschaftsdienst* (7), 463–466.
Witzel, Marc (2012): Medienhandeln, digitale Ungleichheit und Distinktion. *Merz—Zeitschrift für Medienpädagogik* (6), 81–92.
Wu, Chin-Shan & Cheng, Fei-Fei (2011): The Joint Effect of Framing and Anchoring on Internet Buyers' Decision-making. *Electronic Commerce Research and Applications* 10 (3), 358–368.
Yadav, Mayank; Joshi, Yatish & Rahman, Zillur (2015): Mobile Social Media: The New Hybrid Element of Digital Marketing Communications. *Procedia—Social and Behavioral Sciences* 189, 335–343.
Yates, Simeon & Lockley, Eleanor (2018): Social Media and Social Class. *American Behavioral Scientist* 62 (9), 1291–1316.
Zillien, Nicole (2009): *Digitale Ungleichheit. Neue Technologien und alte Ungleichheiten in der Informations- und Wissensgesellschaft*. Wiesbaden: Springer VS.
Zook, Matthew & Graham, Mark (2018): Hacking Code/Space: Confounding the Code of Global Capitalism. *Transactions of the Institute of British Geographers* 42, 1–15.
Zuboff, Shoshana (2015): Big Other: Surveillance Capitalism and the Prospects of an Information Civilion. *Journal of Information Technology* 30, 75–89.
Zuboff, Shoshana (2019): *The Age of Surveillance Capitalism: The Fight for a Human Future at the New Frontier of Power*. London: Profile Books
Zuiderveen Borgesius, Frederik J.; Trilling, Damian; Möller, Judith; Bodó, Balázs; Vreese, Claes H. de & Helberger, Natali (2016): Should We Worry About Filter Bubbles? *Internet Policy Review* 5 (1), 1–11.

SPRINGER NATURE

GPSR Compliance

The European Union's (EU) General Product Safety Regulation (GPSR) is a set of rules that requires consumer products to be safe and our obligations to ensure this.

If you have any concerns about our products, you can contact us on ProductSafety@springernature.com

In case Publisher is established outside the EU, the EU authorized representative is:

Springer Nature Customer Service Center GmbH
Europaplatz 3
69115 Heidelberg, Germany

The manufacturer's authorised representative in the EU is Springer Nature Customer Service Centre GmbH, Europaplatz 3, 69115 Heidelberg, Germany. If you have any concerns regarding our products, please contact ProductSafety@springernature.com

Printed and bound by CPI Group (UK) Ltd, Croydon, CR0 4YY
25/03/2026
02078179-0017